PRESSURE COOKER COOKBOOK
for BEGINNERS

PRESSURE COOKER COOKBOOK *for* BEGINNERS

MAKE THE MOST OF YOUR APPLIANCE AND ENJOY SUPER EASY MEALS

RAMONA CRUZ-PETERS

ROCKRIDGE PRESS

Interior and Cover Designer: Patricia Fabricant
Art Producer: Karen Williams
Editor: Sean Newcott
Production Editor: Andrew Yackira
Photography © Paul Sirisalee, Food styling by Caitlin Haught Brown, Prop Styling by Kimberley Sirisalee and Paul Sirisalee pp. ii, vi, viii, xii, 16, 26, 44, 62, 78, 96, 114, 132, 150, 166, 178; Alamy/Arina Habich (Top Lid) p. 8; Shutterstock pp. 4, 8. Author photo courtesy of © Felicia Reed Photography.

ISBN: Print 978-1-64611-015-5 | eBook 978-1-64611-016-2

R0

TO MY PARENTS,
RAMÓN AND LORRAINE,
FOR INSPIRING MY
LOVE OF COOKING.
TO MY HUSBAND, NIK,
AND SONS, GRAYSON
AND SAWYER, FOR
INDULGING ME.

Contents

Introduction

IT SEEMS LIKE EVERYONE IS JUMPING into the pressure cooker craze. How could you not be tempted to add one to your kitchen when you hear people rave about making a perfectly tender pot roast in a fraction of the time it would take in the slow cooker? While you might be impressed with tackling recipes like roasts in record time, that is just the beginning of how your kitchen will be revolutionized through pressure cooking.

My first experience with pressure cookers was a small stovetop model given to me by my grandmother. I was always impressed by how quickly and flawlessly recipes came out with this simple device, and loved using it for roast beef, rice, and bean dishes. Then, I jumped on the electric multicooker pressure cooker bandwagon. With extra functions, such as sauté mode and programmed settings for dishes like oatmeal, rice, and even yogurt, it was a game changer. Much as with the traditional pressure cooker, every recipe I made in the multicooker turned out perfectly. Meats were tender, sauces were full of flavor—and all in much less time than slow cooking or oven roasting.

But why do you need one? Besides making effortlessly tender meats, pressure cookers have a number of other benefits for busy people who love to cook or wish they were cooking more. They are convenient set-it-and-forget-it devices that cook flavorful meals incredibly quickly. Most of the meals are hands-off once you lock your lid to build the pressure, so pressure cooker dinner recipes are a great fit for even the busiest evening routines. They can also be used for breakfasts, soups, side dishes, and even desserts. With one device that can do so much for a busy person like me, my electric pressure cooker hardly leaves my countertop. It's truly a staple in my kitchen and has practically replaced my other one-off devices like my slow cooker and rice cooker.

Even with all of the aforementioned benefits, as with any new kitchen gadget, the idea of pressure cooking might seem intimidating to beginners. I am here to quell any fears. Even though I am a food and lifestyle blogger for a living, I am all about *easy*. As a busy working mom with an active, on-the-go family, I only have time for recipes that are quick, cost-effective, and tried-and-true delicious (there is no time for a dinner do-over on busy weeknights; we need things that are foolproof). Once you have a basic understanding of how these devices work, you will see, as I did years ago, how pressure cooking changes the game for both seasoned home cooks and beginners.

This book was written with exactly this in mind. Whether you recently scored a great deal on a multicooker or pressure cooker or are thinking of getting one to see what the hype is all about, *Pressure Cooker Cookbook for Beginners* has you covered. I'll walk you through the basics of the two most popular devices (the traditional stovetop pressure cooker and the electric multicooker) so you'll have the confidence you need to start making delicious, easy meals with your own device. Then, along with practical tips, I'll share a variety of easy pressure cooker recipes for every meal and course that even beginners can create. They all use common ingredients, and many will be on your table in 30 minutes or less. Though the best part, in my opinion, is that they are all delicious!

Let this book be your trusty guide on your pressure cooking journey. You'll be serving up fabulous meals in no time and won't be sacrificing any extra time in your busy life to make it happen. I'm excited for you to see the possibilities of what happens after you lock that lid. Happy (pressure) cooking!

1

The ABCs of PRESSURE COOKERS

THE FIRST PRESSURE COOKER was invented by a French physicist in the 1600s, but it wasn't until the 1940s that stovetop models became a popular household appliance. The first electric pressure cooker was patented in 1991, and it was soon followed by programmable models that regulated both time and temperature. The latest wave of multicooker models that sauté, braise, cook, and more, started gaining popularity in the early 2010s, which leads us to the pressure cooking craze of today.

This chapter will help you understand the benefits and functions of pressure cookers (both classic stovetop and electric models), which will alleviate any apprehensions you might have regarding pressure cooking. Once you have the confidence and ability to get the most out of your new kitchen device, you'll be ready to start cooking.

Classic Pressure Cookers

CLASSIC STOVETOP PRESSURE COOKERS have been a staple in American kitchens since World War II. While the science of how they cook food hasn't changed significantly (no need to mess with a good thing), safety and ease of use have improved a lot over the decades. In general, pressure cookers offer an efficient cooking experience that saves time and energy. The rules for pressure cooking are simple: Liquid in the bottom of the pot (whether water below something you're steaming or liquid from your food's sauce itself) is heated, along with the food inside the pot, with an airtight lid locked in place. Since the pot prevents steam from escaping, pressure is created that increases the boiling point of the liquid, cooking the food quickly. As a result, not only do you save time, but you also save energy as foods don't require as much oven or stovetop time under these conditions. The lack of escaping steam from the airtight pot also leads to a cooler kitchen than if you were roasting something in the oven for several hours. This being said, there are many more benefits to pressure cooking than efficient cooking and a cooler kitchen:

Even the toughest meats and dried beans come out perfectly tender when pressure cooked.

Pressure cooking is an especially great method for tougher, cheaper cuts of meat since cooking them under high pressure without letting moisture escape softens them. Similarly, pressure cooking dry beans softens them effortlessly. Purchasing cheaper meats and dry beans is also more economical.

Pressure-cooked food retains more flavor and nutrients during the cooking process.

Compared with steaming or roasting, pressure-cooked food is not only more flavorful but also more nutritious. As the liquids and pan juices can't escape into the air as steam, they are reabsorbed back into the food while it cooks.

Stovetop pressure cookers cook even faster than their electric multicooker counterparts.

Stovetop pressure cookers reach higher pressure levels than electric pressure cookers—an average of 15 pounds per square inch (psi) of pressure, compared with an average range between 10 and 12 psi for popular electric models. In practice, this means that stovetop pressure cookers come to pressure, cook, and release pressure more quickly than electric pressure cookers.

Stovetop pressure cookers can also act and store like a regular pot.

Stovetop models are less bulky than electric models and can be used like a regular stovetop pot in a pinch. This is useful for recipes that call for a sauté phase. Even though stovetop pressure cookers don't have an automated sauté button, they can sauté food directly on the stove, and they store in a cabinet more easily.

Stovetop pressure cookers are cost-effective.

Most of the top-rated stovetop pressure cookers are more reasonably priced than electric multicookers. Along with the fact that you can save money by purchasing cheaper meats and dry beans, stovetop pressure cooking provides a lot of bang for your buck.

STOVETOP PRESSURE COOKER DIAGRAM

Modern stovetop pressure cookers are simpler devices than their electric multicooker counterparts. While there are shape and size variations among stovetop pressure cookers, most of the key components are similar.

1. **Stainless Steel Body.** The main body of most modern stovetop pressure cookers is made of stainless steel or aluminum. I prefer stainless steel pressure cookers, as they are more durable and last longer, though some prefer aluminum as they cook more quickly. The base of the pressure cooker body goes directly on the stovetop burner and works with a variety of stove types. The design enables even heating and can double as a regular pot in addition to pressure cooking.

2. **Stainless Steel Lid.** This heavy-duty lid slides to easily open and close and locks down during cooking to prevent opening the pot prematurely (which could be dangerous). The lid houses several different parts of the device, including the air vent and cover lock, overpressure plug, pressure relief valve, pressure regulator/steam-release valve, and sealing ring.

3. **Handles.** The handles not only let you grip the pressure cooker pot, but they also lock the pot to the lid.

4. **Air Vent/Cover Lock.** Also referred to as a pin, the air vent and cover lock provide a visual indication of the pressure inside the cooker and prevent the lid from being opened until pressure is at a safe level. When the metal pin is all the way at the top, the pot is

at full pressure. The pin will drop completely to indicate that all the pressure has been released.

5. **Overpressure Plug.** This is one of the device's built-in safety mechanisms. If pressure starts to build excessively, it will let off some of the steam to help regulate the device.

6. **Pressure Regulator/Steam-Release Valve.** This is a switch that helps maintain cooking pressure in the pot. When the lever is turned to the pressure setting, it helps keep the pot airtight so that steam doesn't escape. Moving it to the steam-release setting allows steam to leave the pot so it will depressurize. Turning the lever to steam release will provide the "quick release" called for in many pressure cooker recipes.

7. **Sealing Ring.** Sometimes called a gasket, the silicone or rubber sealing ring is one of the most important parts of your pressure cooker. Located on the underside of the lid, it keeps steam in the pot while withstanding a high amount of pressure. If the ring is damaged or not properly placed, both the safety of the pot and its ability to cook could be impacted.

(UNDERSIDE OF THE LID)

FINDING YOUR PERFECT STOVETOP PRESSURE COOKER MODEL

If you're considering purchasing a stovetop pressure cooker, here are some of the highest-rated models on the market. I have ranked them in order of my recommendation; I use the first one on the list (the 8-quart Presto 01370 Stainless Steel Pressure Cooker).

MODEL	SIZE	PROGRAM-MABLE BUTTONS	INCLUDED ACCESSORIES	FEATURES
PRESTO 01370 STAINLESS STEEL PRESSURE COOKER	8 Quart	N/A	Steam basket, recipe book	Multipurpose pot that can stand in as a conventional soup pot. Includes a pop-up pressure indicator, a steam-release mechanism, and an overpressure plug to let off excessive steam. Fully immersible.
PRESTO 01362 STAINLESS STEEL PRESSURE COOKER	6 Quart	N/A	Steam rack, recipe book	Includes a helper handle for easy handling, a pop-up pressure indicator, a steam-release mechanism, and an overpressure plug to let off excessive steam. Dishwasher safe.
T-FAL P25107 PRESSURE COOKER	6.3 Quart	N/A	Steam basket, stand	Variable control valve cooks at 10 or 15 psi for different meals. Includes a pressure indicator, a variable steam-release valve, an overpressure gasket-release window, and the ability to cook multiple foods simultaneously with included accessories.
NUWAVE 31201	6.5 Quart	N/A	N/A	Adjustable pressure level settings and a pressure-release valve.
FISSLER VITAQUICK PRESSURE COOKER	8.5 Quart	N/A	Inset with tripod, wire basket, 2.5 L pressure skillet, extra silicone gasket	Premium model, silent and steam-free, gentle and speed settings, includes a measuring scale and evaporation valve. Dishwasher safe.

Electric Pressure Cookers

THE GAME CHANGED WHEN ELECTRIC PRESSURE COOKERS gained popularity. People rediscovered how effectively and deliciously pressure cooking prepares foods. The time-saving capabilities of cooking under high pressure gave busy people the ability to make delicious roasts with vegetables for dinner without spending all day monitoring the oven. The added versatility of the multicooker digital pressure cookers opened even more recipe options to preparation with the device. Push-button automated settings took much of the guesswork out of pressure cooking, making it a more hands-off approach while still yielding the same results. The machines are smart, adjusting for temperature and pressure level automatically during the phases of pressure cooking, and are designed with multiple safety features.

Electric pressure cookers provide many of the same flavor and time-saving benefits as classic stovetop pressure cookers.

Since the way food is pressure cooked is the same regardless of device type (both cook food at high pressure in an airtight pot), the natural flavor and nutrients of pressure-cooked food are not lost in escaping steam, yielding impossibly tender meats. The primary difference is the amount of pressure in which each type cooks (as described on page 2, it's lower for electric models, which results in longer cooking times than stovetop pressure cooking). Regardless, cook time with an electric pressure cooker is still significantly faster than oven roasting or slow cooking.

Cooking with an electric pressure cooker is a mostly hands-off, set-it-and-forget-it cooking experience.

Electric pressure cookers self-regulate their temperature for the different phases of pressure cooking (coming to pressure, maintaining pressure, and releasing pressure), so once a timer is set, your pot does the work for you. The stovetop version, on the other hand, requires monitoring and manual stove-heat adjustment. Another convenient high-tech feature of these smart pressure cookers is a delayed-start option that allows you to program the device in advance to begin cooking at a designated time.

Electric pressure cookers are considered multicookers as they can do more than just pressure cook.

Aside from sautéing and pressure cooking, many of the popular electric models include modes for slow cooking, cooking rice, and even cooking yogurt, which can allow this single device to replace multiple other single-use devices you may have in your kitchen.

You can expect consistent, quality results when using an electric pressure cooker.

Since heat and pressure are automatic, self-regulated, and timed, you can expect a recipe to work just as well as it did the first time, every time.

Electric pressure cookers are incredibly versatile.

As the name multicooker suggests, these devices can do a whole lot. You can effectively cook nearly every meal or course in your electric pressure cooker, from breakfasts to dips, and breads to roasts, sauces and soups, and even desserts like cheesecake and flan. As you make the recipes in this cookbook, you will see this magic unfold for yourself.

ELECTRIC PRESSURE COOKER DIAGRAM

Since electric pressure cookers are multicooker devices capable of doing more than pressure cooking, they include a few more figurative bells and whistles than stovetop pressure cookers. Here are the standard features you'll find on electric pressure cookers.

1. **Cooker Housing.** This is the outside of the device that contains the electrical components and control panel. This part of the pot is not safe to submerge.
2. **Control Panel.** The control panel has your pot's digital display (for cook timing and messages) and programmable buttons (to choose cooking settings and start or stop cooking modes).
3. **Inner Pot.** The inner pot is the removable stainless steel pot where you cook your food. It is often safe to submerge and may even be dishwasher safe. It includes fill-level lines so you don't overfill the pot.
4. **Exterior Pot.** The removable inner pot sits inside of a metal pot attached to the cooker housing. This is the exterior pot and should not be cooked in directly.
5. **Heating Element.** At the bottom of the exterior pot is the heating element. This is much like a stove burner and will heat your inner pot to sauté and bring the pot to pressure.

(UNDERSIDE
OF THE LID)

(INSIDE
THE POT)

(INSIDE
THE POT)

(INSIDE
THE POT)

6. **Condensation Collector.** This catches excess moisture so that it won't drip onto your counter. I have rarely seen this become full, so you may not need to clean it every time you use the pot. It is mainly for convenience and doesn't impact cooking.

7. **Lid.** A key part of your electric pressure cooker, the lid locks safely into place before bringing your pot to pressure. It also houses the steam-release mechanism, float valve, and sealing ring.

8. **Lid Handle.** The lid handle helps you turn and lift the lid as needed.

9. **Steam Release.** This switch, sometimes called a "pressure-release button" will be used nearly every time you pressure cook. The removable switch, which feels loose (that's normal), can be turned to sealing or venting. When in sealing, the pot is kept airtight so pressure can build inside. Moving it to venting allows steam (and pressure) to escape and is what you will do when a recipe calls for a quick release of pressure.

10. **Float Valve.** Sometimes called a "pin," this small metal float valve is the visual indicator if there is pressure in the pot or not. When the pin is all the way at the top, the pot is at full pressure. The pin will drop completely to indicate that all the pressure has been released and the pot is safe to open.

11. **Sealing Ring.** The silicone or rubber sealing ring (sometimes called a gasket) is one of the most important parts of your pressure cooker. Located on the underside of the lid, it enables the pot to become airtight while withstanding a high amount of pressure to prevent steam from escaping. If the ring is damaged or not properly in place, it will affect your pot's ability to cook and the safety of your device.

FINDING YOUR PERFECT ELECTRIC PRESSURE COOKER MODEL

If you're looking to purchase an electric pressure cooker, you've no doubt heard about the number-one-selling Instant Pot. I personally use and recommend the 6-quart Instant Pot Duo Plus but have had the opportunity to try a few other devices that are also solid choices. I have ranked my top five electric pressure cooker models.

MODEL	SIZE	PROGRAMMABLE BUTTONS	INCLUDED ACCESSORIES	FEATURES
INSTANT POT DUO PLUS	6 Quart	15 cooking presets: Soup/Broth, Meat/Stew, Bean/Chili, Cake, Egg, Slow Cook, Sauté/Simmer, Rice Cook, Multigrain, Porridge, Steam, Sterilize, Yogurt, Keep Warm, and Pressure Cook	Steam rack/trivet with handles, serving spoon, soup spoon, measuring cup	Can replace up to 9 kitchen appliances, includes a delayed-start timer option
INSTANT POT LUX	6 Quart	12 cooking presets: Soup/Broth, Meat/Stew, Cake, Egg, Slow Cook, Sauté, Rice Cook, Multigrain, Porridge, Steam, Keep Warm, and Pressure Cook	Steam rack/trivet, serving spoon, soup spoon	Can replace up to 6 kitchen appliances, includes a delayed-start timer option
MEALTHY MULTI-POT	6 Quart	14 cooking presets: Poultry, Meat/Stew, Bean/Chili, Soup, Sauté/Simmer, Cake, Rice, Multigrain, Porridge, Steam, Slow Cook, Keep Warm, Yogurt, and Pressure Cook	Extra silicone gasket, silicone mitts, steamer basket, steam rack/trivet, ladle, rice paddle, and measuring cup	Can replace up to 9 kitchen appliances, includes a delayed-start timer option
CROCK-POT EXPRESS CROCK PROGRAMMABLE MULTICOOKER	6 Quart	8 cooking presets: Meat/Stew, Beans/Chili, Rice/Risotto, Yogurt, Poultry, Dessert, Soup, and Multigrain	Recipe book, steaming rack, and serving spoon	Can replace up to 8 kitchen appliances from the brand leader in one-pot cooking, includes a delayed-start timer option
MUELLER ULTRAPOT	6 Quart	15 cooking presets: Oatmeal, Broth/Soup, Poultry, Yogurt, Egg, Beans/Chili, Rice, Pressure Cook, Cake, Slow Cook, Steam, Sauté, Canning, and Multigrain	Tempered glass lid, measuring cup, spoon, steamer basket, extra silicone gasket	Can replace up to 10 kitchen appliances, includes a delayed-start timer option, can cook 2 dishes simultaneously with included accessories

How to Make the Most of Your Pressure Cooker

ANY NEW KITCHEN GADGET CAN SEEM INTIMIDATING AT FIRST—especially one that cooks at high pressure—but with a little knowledge you'll be confidently making recipes in your pressure cooker, always with safety in mind.

» **Are electric models better than stovetop models?**

Both types of pressure cookers get the job done well since they use the same method of cooking food under pressure. Each model has its pros and cons. Stovetop pressure cookers are faster overall (they cook at higher pressure than electric models) but require more "babysitting" since you must manually adjust the stove burner. Electric pressure cookers are more hands-off, adjusting temperature and pressure automatically. You can sauté food in both models, but electric pressure cookers offer several more cooking functions, like rice cooking and slow cooking.

» **What size pressure cooker do I need?**

This depends on the number of people you are serving. Here are the common sizes of pressure cookers and how many people each accommodates:

* **3-QUART (MINI PRESSURE COOKERS):** Ideal for 2 people
* **6-QUART (THE MOST POPULAR):** Works well for 4 to 6 people
* **8-QUART (THE SECOND MOST POPULAR):** Ideal for larger families or groups

NOTE: Most pressure cooker accessories are made for the 6- and 8-quart sizes.

» **Do pressure cookers really cook food faster?**

While total cook time in a pressure cooker is often faster than oven cooking and significantly faster than slow cooking, cook time can sometimes be misleading. It's important to note that there is a difference between cooking time and total time, as it can take 5 to 25 minutes for the pot to reach pressure before the cooking time starts, then 8 to 30 minutes for pressure to release from the pot naturally (if natural pressure release is required). Therefore, when you see that a whole chicken cooks in 20 minutes, this doesn't include the amount of time to come to or release pressure, which could add another 30 minutes to the total time.

» **Is it safe to use a pressure cooker?**

Newer models of both stovetop and electric pressure cookers are equipped with redundant safety measures for added caution and are much safer than old mid-century models. Your biggest safety risk are burns from steam or hot stainless steel components. See the list of safety DOs and DON'Ts on page 13 and be sure to follow them every time you use a pressure cooker.

>> **Are stovetop pressure cookers dangerous?**

You may have heard stories of split pea soup explosions in your grandma's kitchen with her older pressure cooker model. It's important to monitor stovetop pressure cookers while they cook, reduce the stove's burner heat when they reach pressure, and follow usage guidelines. If you adhere to the safety DOs and DON'Ts listed on page 13 every time you use a pressure cooker, there is a very low chance of unwittingly reenacting that scene from *The Exorcist*.

>> **I see a lot of unfamiliar acronyms and terminology in pressure cooker recipes. What do they mean?**

Some of them may become apparent by reading the parts descriptions in the diagrams (see pages 3 and 7), but yes, pressure cooking recipe writers do use some specific jargon that may be unfamiliar at first. Here are the most common acronyms and terms used in pressure cooking recipes and what they mean:

* **PIP:** Stands for "pot in pot," which is a method by which a smaller pot or bowl of food is placed inside the pressure cooker pot. This is a gentler cooking method and is common for foods that you can't cook directly in liquid, such as breads or desserts.
* **NPR OR NATURAL RELEASE:** NPR stands for "natural pressure release." This refers to allowing pressure to release from the pot on its own slowly while the steam-release switch is still in the sealing position.
* **QR:** The "quick-release" method is for releasing pressure from the pot quickly by moving the switch to the venting position.

>> **My steam-release switch seems loose; is that normal? Is it okay for steam to leak from it?**

Yes, it should feel loose. It's also normal for some steam to escape from it while cooking (especially with stovetop pressure cookers). This is a safety measure of the device to regulate pressure. As long as the lid is securely locked, the switch is set to sealing, and steam is not escaping from somewhere else on the pot (around the lid, for example), this is normal.

Pressure Cooking with Confidence and Caution

Modern pressure cookers (both stovetop and electric) are equipped with more safety features than the pressure cookers of yesteryear, but as they operate with very high heat and generate pounds of pressure internally, it's important to adhere to some key safety rules for operating them.

>> **DO** use an oven mitt or a wooden spoon to release pressure with the release switch. Moving the switch will release hot steam from inside the cooker and could burn your hand. For the same reason, release the steam away from your face or anything you wouldn't want damaged with a blast of hot steam.

>> **DO** include the required amount of liquid in your pot per the recipe (usually 1 cup or more). If there is no liquid, the pot will be unable to create steam to pressure cook the food and this could lead to a scorched pot.

>> **DO** properly clean your pot after every use, including the valves and gaskets. If they become clogged, a safety mechanism may not be able to regulate pressure or create warnings, and your food may not cook properly.

>> **DO** follow trusted recipes when trying something new, as you won't be familiar with how your device will react. For example, starchy foods (like split peas, rice, and pastas) expand a lot and tend to froth. If the pot is overfilled or the recipe is not closely followed, froth can block the pressure release safety valves.

>> **DO** open the lid away from you to avoid steam burns.

>> **DO** ensure curious kids and other family members are aware of all these tips, and never leave stovetop pressure cookers unattended.

>> **DON'T** cook without inspecting the key parts of the device, such as the inner sealing ring and lid. If the ring is damaged or not attached properly, your pot may not effectively seal and therefore may not cook your food properly. The lid should be on straight and securely locked into place—otherwise, as pressure builds, the lid could come off with quite a bit of force.

>> **DON'T** attempt to unlock or open the lid without releasing pressure first. The pot is filled with hot steam and pounds of pressure! Newer stovetop and electric pressure cookers typically have mechanisms that won't allow you to unlock the lid while there is pressure in the pot, but still, don't attempt it.

>> **DON'T** overfill your pot. Adhere to guidelines for your specific pot size and reduce your recipe ingredients if needed. Overfilling can result in your venting components becoming clogged, which would disengage the cooker's safety mechanism.

>> **DON'T** submerge your electric pressure cooker housing in water. Only the inner pot can be submerged.

>> **DON'T** use your pressure cooker for "pressure frying." These pots are not meant to deep fry under pressure, and this could result in fire and explosions.

>> **DON'T** buy a used pressure cooker. They may not be safe since you can't trust the integrity of all the parts.

Cleaning and Caring for Your Pressure Cooker

IF YOU WANT SOMETHING TO LAST, you've got to take care of it. Keeping your pressure cooker in good shape will have it performing well for years to come. This includes keeping all parts clean and regularly inspected. Cleaning and inspecting your pressure cooker is important not only for health and safety (to avoid bacterial growth in the nooks and crevices) but also for maintaining the integrity of the device (cooking can and will be impacted if the sealing ring or valves are damaged or blocked by stuck-on food). After cleaning, don't store your pressure cooker until it is dry, and store it with the lid upside down over the pot (and not sealed).

How to Clean Classic Pressure Cookers

Since they don't have electric parts, stovetop pressure cookers are easier to clean. Some parts may even be dishwasher safe (consult your manufacturer's instructions).

* I always recommend cleaning the pot and lid while they are still warm but safe to handle. This makes it easier to clean, and limiting the amount of time with caked-on food on the pot will keep the metal shape intact over time.
* If necessary (and if it is okay per manufacturer instructions), soak the inside of the pot with water for hardened food and use the abrasive side of a sponge or a plastic scouring pad (avoid metal scouring pads that could damage the pot).
* Clean the gasket and valves to get rid of hidden grime every time you clean your pressure cooker.

How to Clean Electric Pressure Cookers

Be sure to unplug your electric pressure cooker before you attempt to clean it, and only submerge parts that are safe to submerge per your manufacturer's instructions. The housing should not be submerged, but the outside can be wiped down with a damp cloth or sponge. The inner pot and ring are often safe to submerge, but consult your specific model's instructions to be sure.

* I recommend cleaning the inner pot while it is still warm but safe to handle, as it will be easier to clean.
* For caked-on food, if it is okay per the manufacturer instructions, fill the inner pot with water to let soak, then use the abrasive side of a sponge or a plastic scouring pad (avoid metal scouring pads as they could damage the pot).
* Clean the valves to get rid of hidden grime, and inspect and clean the sealing ring every time you clean your pressure cooker.
* If the ring is damaged or shows wear and tear like cracks or deformation, cooking will be affected.
* The sealing ring also absorbs flavor, so carefully remove it to clean it thoroughly after use, and perhaps buy an extra sealing ring to keep on hand specifically for cooking aromatic dishes, like curry (see my list of recommended accessories for your pressure cooker on page 20).
* To rid your electric pressure cooker of especially strong lingering odors, add 2 cups of white vinegar to your pot and run it on the Steam setting for 2 minutes, then clean normally.
* Occasionally clean the condensation collector (as it is not always needed).

2

PRESSURE COOKERS
for COOKING
PERFECTION

NOW THAT YOU KNOW the many benefits of pressure cookers (and how to use them safely and with confidence), it's time to put your device to use. Regardless of whether you have a stovetop or electric pressure cooker, you'll be amazed at the variety of foods that you can prepare with one: The pressure cooker seems to do it all. This chapter will prepare you to make these delicious recipes and more with lists of kitchen staples you should have on hand (many are common household ingredients that you likely have in your pantry already), the pressure cooker tools and accessories that I recommend, and step-by-step instructions for using your stovetop or electric pressure cooker.

Prepping the Kitchen

ONE OF THE BIGGEST BENEFITS of pressure cookers (especially electronic multi-cookers) is their ability to act as a stand-alone, all-in-one kitchen appliance that can take the place of numerous other one-off devices. This is great for beginner cooks as well as those who don't have a lot of kitchen space. With a good pressure cooker and some key ingredients and tools, you don't need a lot of time, space, or energy to create meals that seem like you've spent all day preparing them. Here are items I recommend keeping on hand.

SIMPLE STAPLES

Eggs. Whether hard-boiled or used in breakfast casseroles, pressure cookers cook eggs to perfection.

Milk. From oatmeal to mains to desserts, this multiuse ingredient is always useful.

Heavy cream. When you need a richer, creamier sauce, heavy cream is a better choice than milk.

Plain, unsweetened yogurt. Yogurt makes pressure cooker breads and cakes light and fluffy.

Real unsalted butter. Sweet breakfasts and desserts always come out better using real, unsalted butter.

Cornstarch. Adding a mixture of cornstarch and water after pressure cooking is a great way to thicken sauces.

Baking powder and baking soda. These are perfect for making "baked" goods in your pressure cooker.

Honey. Honey helps thicken sauces made in your pressure cooker.

Flour, sugar, and brown sugar. All home cooks should keep these on hand.

Bread crumbs. Bread crumbs can bind meatballs and create crumb toppings.

Oats. Keep quick and/or old-fashioned oats on hand for oatmeal and crumble toppings.

Chicken broth. Canned, boxed, or homemade broth makes sauces, rice, and steamed dishes more savory.

Vegetable oil, olive oil, and toasted sesame oil. These are the ultimate three oils to have stocked.

Soy sauce or tamari. Use for Asian-style recipes and additions to meat marinades.

Garlic. Keep a fresh bulb of garlic at room temperature to grab cloves as needed.

HERBS AND SPICES

Salt. I recommend stocking both table salt and coarse (kosher) salt.

Pepper. Keep both ground black pepper and whole peppercorns to crack in a pepper mill.

Garlic powder. I use garlic powder in almost every savory recipe.

Onion powder. This often-forgotten spice can really take a sauce to the next level.

Dried basil, oregano, parsley, thyme, and rosemary. These herbs can be used in combination to create many different flavors.

Dried sage. Sage is one of my favorite flavors for poultry or pork and side dishes served with poultry.

Bay leaves. These are essential for soups, stews, and some pasta sauces.

Chili powder. From mild to spicy, chili powder adds color and flavor to beans, stews, chilies, and meats.

Ground cumin. Cumin is used in many Latin American dishes and pairs deliciously with black beans.

Cajun seasoning. Use this to add flavor and spice to beans, stews, and seafood.

Paprika. Just a bit of paprika adds color and bold flavor to many dishes.

Ground ginger. Ground ginger (or grated fresh ginger) adds incredible flavor.

Ground cinnamon. A little cinnamon goes a long way in sweet breakfast and dessert dishes.

TOOLS

You can do a lot with pressure cookers, but you can do even more with a few extra tools and accessories. Here are the tools that get the most use in my kitchen and will be helpful to you as you create the recipes in this cookbook. You can find sets on Amazon that bundle many of these together at a savings.

Steamer rack trivet. Use this accessory to raise food or inner bowls that you don't want to sit directly in the liquid at the bottom of the pot.

Steamer basket with dividers. This is useful for smaller vegetables and foods that would otherwise fall between the slats in a trivet.

7-cup heat-safe bowl (such as a glass Pyrex bowl). This size fits perfectly inside a 6- or 8-quart pressure cooker for making pot-in-pot recipes. If you have a smaller pressure cooker model, make sure to check the dimensions of your inner pot before buying one.

Silicone egg-bite mold. These are not just for making egg bites, but also muffins and other recipes in individual-size portions.

7-inch springform pan. Several pressure cooker recipes call for a springform pan (not just the famous pressure cooker cheesecake). This size is ideal for 6- or 8-quart pots.

6-cup Bundt pan. The shape of the Bundt pan cooks cakes and breads differently than a springform or glass bowl inside your pressure cooker and is a good option to own. The 6-cup size fits nicely inside 6- and 8-quart pressure cookers.

Aluminum foil. Foil is useful for covering things as needed and creating slings to lift inner bowls out of your pressure cooker.

Wooden spoon and silicone-tipped tongs. These will help you sauté and move food without scratching the inside of your pot.

Oven mitts. Your regular oven mitts will work, but the smaller "pinch" mitts are especially helpful when pulling hot slings and trivets out of your pot, or when lifting out the still-hot inner pot from your electric pressure cooker to clean it.

Extra sealing rings. As mentioned in chapter 1, since the inner sealing ring from your pressure cooker lid absorbs flavor, it's helpful to have a few extra so you can designate different rings for savory and sweet recipes.

Bakeware sling. I love having one of these trivet-and-sling-in-one tools. While you can do the same with a foil sling and a steamer rack trivet, the convenience of this sling garners a lot of use.

Stackable egg steamer racks. If you make hard-boiled eggs frequently (and you will when you see how perfectly they come out in the pressure cooker), this may be a good investment. Otherwise you can arrange eggs on a steamer rack trivet.

The Stovetop Pressure Cooker, Step by Step

PREPARING MEALS IN A STOVETOP PRESSURE COOKER is pretty simple, as these devices do not have as many features as electric multicooker pressure cookers. Once you understand how to carry out the basic steps for cooking in one, you should be able to follow any pressure cooker recipe. Here is an example of how to cook something on the steamer rack trivet in your stovetop pressure cooker, such as a vegetable, or a piece of meat that doesn't cook in a sauce.

1. Place the steamer rack trivet in the bottom of your pressure cooker, then pour in the amount of liquid stated in the recipe. The liquid should be at room temperature, as liquid that is too cold or too hot will require different amounts of time to come to pressure, which could affect how the food cooks.

2. Place the food on top of the trivet, then seal and lock the lid in place.

3. Make sure the pressure regulator/steam-release valve is set to "pressure," then turn the burner to high heat.

4. Your pot will be at full pressure when the metal pin is all the way at the top. This is when your pressure cooking time begins. You will then lower the burner heat to maintain pressure (do not keep the burner on high heat). If you have a gas stove, turn the flame to low. If you have an electric cooktop, the burner will not cool down quickly enough, so I recommend a two-burner method: While the pot is on one burner over high heat waiting to come to pressure, start heating a second burner on low heat. When the pot reaches pressure, carefully move the pot to the burner on low heat for the remainder of the cook time. You will know pressure is maintained if the pin stays up while the burner is on low.

5. When the cook time ends, remove the pressure cooker from the heat. If the recipe calls for a certain number of minutes of natural pressure release, set a timer for that amount of time and leave the lid on the pot and unaltered until time is up. After that time (or right after removing from the heat if the recipe calls for a quick release of pressure), move the pressure regulator/steam-release valve to "steam release." Once the pressure has released completely (you will see and hear the pin drop), you can unlock and remove the lid.

Stovetop Pressure Cooking Tips

Sautéing. If a recipe calls for sautéing before or after pressure cooking, you can do this directly in the pot over a burner, just as you would in a skillet or saucepan.

Pot-in-pot (PIP) method. This is a gentler cooking method where a smaller pot or bowl is placed inside the pressure cooker pot. It is common to use for breads or desserts where you can't cook the food directly in liquid, or for thick sauces that may be susceptible to burning if cooked directly in the pot for a long period.

Preventing steam eruptions. When cooking frothy, thick, or fatty foods under pressure, occasionally a bubble or pocket of high-pressure steam gets stuck under the surface. To avoid these popping and causing food eruptions after the lid has been removed, tap or lightly shake the pot before opening it. You should also never use quick release for thick and froth-prone foods like applesauce and lentils.

The Electric Pressure Cooker, Step by Step

COOKING WITH AN ELECTRIC PRESSURE COOKER is very hands-off, thanks to automatic temperature and pressure adjustments. Specific settings can also take some of the guesswork out of the time to prepare certain types of foods. Here is an example of how to cook something on the steamer rack trivet in your electric pressure cooker, like larger vegetables or meat that doesn't cook in a sauce.

1. Place the steamer rack trivet in the bottom of your pressure cooker's inner pot, then add the amount of liquid stated in the recipe to the bottom. The liquid should be at room temperature, as liquid that is too cold or too hot will require different amounts of time to come to pressure, which could affect how the food cooks (as food begins cooking while the pot comes to pressure).

2. Place the food on top of the trivet, then seal and lock the lid in place.

3. Make sure the steam-release switch is set to "sealing," then push the pressure cook button (this button is labeled as "manual" on some models) and adjust the cooking time according to the recipe. The cooking time will begin automatically when the pot has reached pressure, and a timer will begin counting down.

4. When the cook time ends, the electric pressure cooker will beep and turn off the heat automatically. If the recipe calls for natural pressure release, watch the timer on the pot (which will start going up in time at this point) and leave the lid on the pot and unaltered for the stated amount of time. After that time (or after the cooking time ends, if the recipe calls for a quick release of pressure), move the steam-release switch to venting. Once the pressure has released completely (you will see and hear the pin drop), you can unlock and remove the lid.

Electric Pressure Cooking Tips

Sautéing. If a recipe calls for sautéing before or after pressure cooking, you can do this in the inner pot by pressing the sauté button. Be sure to press the cancel button when you're done.

Pot-in-Pot (PIP) method. In this method, a smaller pot or bowl is placed inside the pressure cooker pot. It's a gentler cooking method and is common for breads or desserts where you can't cook the food directly in liquid, or for thick sauces that may be susceptible to burning if cooked directly in the pot for a long period.

Increasing or decreasing the recipe quantity. Changing the recipe quantity is easy to do as long as your pot contents are safely below the max fill line. The cook time usually remains the same, though the amount of time to come to pressure may vary slightly.

Preventing steam eruptions. When cooking frothy, thick, or fatty foods under pressure, occasionally a bubble or pocket of high-pressure steam gets stuck under the surface. To prevent these from popping and causing food eruptions after the lid has been removed, I usually tap or lightly shake the pot before opening it. You should also never use quick release for thick or froth-prone foods like applesauce or lentils.

Cook time variance. Different electric pressure cooker models (even from the same brand) can have cook time variance depending on their size, heat and pressure levels, and sensitivity to heat for the burn error message. You will get to know your own device after some experience using it and may find that your device consistently requires a few more or less minutes of cook time than a recipe states.

CONVERT COOK TIMES WITH EASE

STOVETOP PRESSURE COOKERS TEND TO COME to pressure and cook a little faster than electric models (stovetop pressure cookers cook at an average of 15 psi, or pounds per square inch, of pressure, compared with an average range between 10 and 12 psi for popular electric models). In this cookbook, most recipes are written to work in either an electric or stovetop model, with variations noted when there are large differences in cooking time. For foods that shouldn't be over-done (for preference or practicality), some rules of thumb for converting recipe cook times for a stovetop pressure cooker follow.

Keep an eye on your stovetop pressure cooker until it comes to pressure so you can set a timer right when pressure cooking begins.

* **For recipes with less than 10 minutes of cook time, reduce the time by 1 minute.**
* **For recipes with 11–20 minutes of cook time, reduce the time by 2 minutes.**
* **For recipes with 20 minutes of cook time or more, reduce the time by 5 minutes.**

If your food isn't cooked as much as you'd like after cooking ends and pressure is released, you can always put the lid back on, bring back to pressure, and cook for a few additional minutes.

It is important to note that different models of electric pressure cookers can have cook time variance depending on multiple factors. You will become familiar with your own device after some experience using it, and if you find that foods consistently require a few extra minutes, you may want to automatically increase cooking time when trying new recipes.

Pressure Cooking with Confidence: Navigating the Recipes

IN THIS COOKBOOK YOU'LL FIND RECIPES for breakfast, snacks and appetizers, vegetables and sides, meat main dishes, beans and rice, pasta, stews, soups, and desserts—75 in total. All these recipes were developed with the beginner in mind, so I kept them simple and easy, without sacrificing any flavor. Better yet, about half of them can be prepared in 30 minutes or less!

As you go through the recipes, you will see that many include substitution options. You will also find clear cooking and prep times, including the time it will take for the recipe to come to pressure, so that you'll know exactly how long each recipe will take from start to finish. The recipe section is also full of tips for using the pressure cooker, along with tweaks and shortcuts to customize individual recipes. Each recipe includes nutritional information to help you plan around any dietary needs.

Now that you're primed on how to use your pressure cooker, you're ready to get cooking! Gather your pressure cooker, your accessories, your ingredients and spices, and (most importantly) your taste buds and belly, and get cooking!

3

BREAKFAST

5-Ingredient Cinnamon and Brown Sugar Oatmeal

30 MINUTES · NUT-FREE · VEGETARIAN · SERVES 2

PREP TIME: 5 minutes

TOTAL COOK TIME:
25 minutes

APPROX. PRESSURE BUILD:
7 to 8 minutes

PRESSURE COOK: 6 minutes

PRESSURE RELEASE:
10 minutes

2 cups water, divided

1 cup old-fashioned oats

¾ cup milk

2 tablespoons brown sugar

½ teaspoon ground cinnamon

This hands-off oatmeal is a great breakfast for busy mornings. My youngest son is such a big fan of this oatmeal that he asks for it every chance he can get. It's very easy to make, and the foolproof pot-in-pot cooking method cooks the oats evenly and gently. If you like, serve the oatmeal topped with Fresh Berry Compote (page 177) or sliced fresh fruit, or stir in some cream.

1. Pour 1 cup of water into the pressure cooker pot and place a steamer rack trivet in the bottom.
2. In a heat-safe bowl (I use a 7-cup glass bowl), stir together the remaining 1 cup of water, oats, milk, brown sugar, and cinnamon.
3. Place the bowl on the trivet.
4. Close and lock the pressure cooker lid, make sure the pressure/steam-release switch is set to sealing, and set the cooking time to 6 minutes at high/normal pressure (if using an electric pressure cooker; for stovetop pressure cookers, heat over a burner on high heat, set a timer for 6 minutes after the pot has reached pressure, then reduce the heat to low). It will take 7 to 8 minutes for the pot to come to pressure with an electric pressure cooker and 4 to 5 minutes to come to pressure with a stovetop pressure cooker before the cooking time begins.

COOKING TIPS

✳ This recipe will yield oatmeal with a firm texture. For softer, mushier oatmeal, increase the pressure cook time by 2 minutes.

✳ If you have a bakeware sling, you can use that to lower the bowl into the pressure cooker. If not, you can create your own sling by placing a long strip of aluminum foil under the bowl and folding the ends up above the bowl as makeshift handles. Either method will make it easier to remove the bowl from the pot after cooking.

5. After the pressure cooking time ends, electric pressure cookers will automatically turn off their heat (stovetop pressure cookers must be removed from the heat). Allow the pressure to release from the pot naturally for 10 minutes before releasing the remaining pressure using the manufacturer's quick-release method.

6. Remove the bowl from the pressure cooker and stir. The oatmeal will thicken as it cools.

PER SERVING: Calories: 231; Total Fat: 5g; Saturated Fat: 2g; Cholesterol: 8mg; Sodium: 48mg; Carbohydrates: 41g; Fiber: 4g; Protein: 8g

Loaded Cheesy Bacon Grits

30 MINUTES • GLUTEN-FREE • NUT-FREE • SERVES 4

PREP TIME: 5 minutes

TOTAL COOK TIME:
30 minutes

APPROX. PRESSURE BUILD:
8 to 9 minutes

PRESSURE COOK: 15 minutes

PRESSURE RELEASE:
5 minutes

3 cups water, divided

1½ cups milk

1 cup quick grits (not instant grits)

¼ teaspoon salt

½ cup shredded cheddar cheese

¼ cup real bacon bits

2 tablespoons unsalted butter, at room temperature

1 tablespoon chopped fresh chives

In Texas, grits can be sweet, savory, cheesy, part of a breakfast, or a side dish for barbecue. Our family's favorite way to eat them is "loaded" like a baked potato, mixed with cheese, bacon, and chives. Feel free to customize the toppings in this recipe to your taste or leave them off and just stir in some milk and sugar.

1. Pour 1 cup of water into the pressure cooker pot and place a steamer rack trivet in the bottom.
2. In a heat-safe bowl (I use a 7-cup glass bowl), stir together the remaining 2 cups of water, milk, grits, and salt.
3. Place the bowl on the trivet.
4. Close and lock the pressure cooker lid, make sure the pressure/steam-release switch is set to sealing, and set the cooking time to 15 minutes at high/normal pressure (if using an electric pressure cooker; for stovetop pressure cookers, heat over a burner on high heat, set a timer for 15 minutes after the pot has reached pressure, then reduce the heat to low). It will take 8 to 9 minutes for the pot to come to pressure before the cooking time begins.

COOKING TIPS

* This recipe makes thick grits, as that is how my family likes them. If you prefer thinner grits, add an additional ½ cup water or milk.

* See the Cooking Tip on page 29 for how to use a bakeware sling.

5. After the pressure cooking time ends, electric pressure cookers will automatically turn off their heat (stovetop pressure cookers must be removed from the heat). Allow the pressure to release from the pot naturally for 5 minutes before releasing the remaining pressure using the manufacturer's quick-release method.

6. Remove the bowl from the pressure cooker and stir. The grits will thicken as they cool.

7. Stir in the cheese, bacon bits, butter, and chives.

PER SERVING: Calories: 317; Total Fat: 14g; Saturated Fat: 8g; Cholesterol: 43mg; Sodium: 540mg; Carbohydrates: 36g; Fiber: 2g; Protein: 13g

Ham and Cheese Egg Bites

30 MINUTES • GLUTEN-FREE • KETO • NUT-FREE • SERVES 7

PREP TIME: 5 minutes

TOTAL COOK TIME:
25 minutes

APPROX. PRESSURE BUILD:
7 to 8 minutes

PRESSURE COOK: 11 minutes

PRESSURE RELEASE:
5 minutes

Nonstick cooking spray

1 cup water

4 large eggs

½ cup chopped ham

½ cup shredded
cheddar cheese

¼ cup cottage cheese

½ tablespoon chopped
fresh parsley

¼ teaspoon garlic powder

¼ teaspoon salt

¼ teaspoon freshly ground
black pepper

These are reminiscent of the popular sous-vide egg bites and can be modified endlessly with different meat, cheese, and vegetable combinations (think bacon, sausage, Gruyère cheese, pepper Jack cheese, bell pepper, spinach, tomatoes, and more). They are also great for meal prepping, as you can make up to 14 at a time and store them in the refrigerator for a few days.

1. Spray the cups of a silicone egg mold with nonstick cooking spray.
2. Pour the water into the pressure cooker pot and place a steamer rack trivet in the bottom.
3. In a medium bowl, whisk the eggs. Stir in the ham, cheddar cheese, cottage cheese, parsley, garlic powder, salt, and pepper until well mixed.
4. Divide the egg mixture evenly into the seven egg-bite mold cups. Place the egg-bite mold on the trivet.
5. Close and lock the pressure cooker lid, make sure the pressure/steam-release switch is set to sealing, and set the cooking time to 11 minutes at high/normal pressure (if using an electric pressure cooker; for stovetop pressure cookers, heat over a burner on high heat, set a timer for 11 minutes after the pot has reached pressure, then reduce the heat to low). It will take 7 to 8 minutes for the pot to come to pressure before the cooking time begins (it may be faster for stovetop pressure cookers).

If you're not a fan of the texture of cottage cheese, you can
substitute the same amount of
heavy cream.

6. After the pressure cooking time ends, electric pressure cookers will automatically turn off their heat (stovetop pressure cookers must be removed from the heat). Allow the pressure to release from the pot naturally for 5 minutes before releasing the remaining pressure using your manufacturer's quick-release method.

7. Remove the mold from the pressure cooker and cool on a wire rack before using a spoon or butter knife to remove the egg bites from the mold.

PER SERVING: Calories: 93; Total Fat: 7g; Saturated Fat: 3g; Cholesterol: 121mg; Sodium: 315mg; Carbohydrates: 1g; Fiber: 0g; Protein: 8g

COOKING TIP

If you have two silicone egg bite molds, you can double this recipe and cook both batches at the same time by laying a piece of aluminum foil on one mold and placing the other mold on top of it (do not wrap the bottom mold with foil, just place the foil between the two to prevent excess water from the top mold getting into the cups of the bottom mold). The cooking time will remain the same.

Sausage and Spinach Quiche

GLUTEN-FREE • KETO • NUT-FREE • SERVES 4 TO 6

PREP TIME: 10 minutes

TOTAL COOK TIME:
50 minutes

APPROX. PRESSURE BUILD:
6 to 7 minutes

PRESSURE COOK:
30 minutes

PRESSURE RELEASE:
10 minutes

8 ounces ground sausage

¼ cup finely chopped onion

6 large eggs

½ cup heavy cream

1½ cups chopped spinach

¼ cup Parmesan cheese

¼ teaspoon garlic powder

¼ teaspoon salt

¼ teaspoon freshly ground black pepper

½ cup chopped tomato

1 cup water

Nonstick cooking spray

This hearty crustless quiche is impressive enough for brunch guests yet easy to make. You can customize this keto-friendly breakfast by adding or swapping meat, cheese, and vegetables to create unlimited variations. For example, chopped cooked ham or bacon can be substituted for the sausage. Gruyère, Asiago, and Jack cheeses are delicious in quiche if you'd like to try something different than Parmesan. You can also add nearly any vegetable of your choice.

1. Select the sauté function on the pressure cooker (if using an electric pressure cooker; for stovetop pressure cookers, heat over a burner on medium-high heat). When the pot is hot, add the ground sausage and chopped onion and sauté until the sausage is browned and cooked through, 8 to 10 minutes. Press cancel or turn off the burner. Transfer the sausage and onion mixture to a paper towel–lined plate and set aside to drain. Wipe out the inside of the pressure cooker pot when it is cool enough to handle.

2. In a medium bowl, whisk together the eggs and heavy cream. Stir in the spinach, Parmesan cheese, garlic powder, salt, and pepper until well blended.

3. Add the sausage and onion mixture to the egg mixture, along with the tomato, and stir well.

4. Pour the water into the pressure cooker pot and place a steamer rack trivet in the bottom.

INGREDIENT TIP

If you decide to make this without spinach or tomatoes, your quiche will not be as moist (as both spinach and tomatoes release liquid while cooking). You can make up for this by adding two more table-spoons of heavy cream. Any type of milk can be substituted for heavy cream if you want a lighter variation.

COOKING TIPS

* The recipe calls for a soufflé dish, but you can also use a heat-safe glass bowl or a 7-inch springform pan lined with aluminum foil.

* See the Cooking Tip on page 29 for how to use a bakeware sling.

5. Spray a soufflé dish with nonstick cooking spray (make sure the dish can fit inside your pressure cooker pot). Pour the egg mixture into the prepared souffle dish and cover loosely with aluminum foil.

6. Place the dish on the trivet inside the pot.

7. Close and lock the pressure cooker lid, make sure the pressure/steam-release switch is set to sealing, and set the cooking time to 30 minutes at high/normal pressure (if using an electric pressure cooker; for stovetop pressure cookers, heat over a burner on high heat, set a timer for 30 minutes after the pot has reached pressure, then reduce the heat to low). It will take 6 to 7 minutes for the pot to come to pressure before cooking time begins.

8. After the pressure cooking time ends, electric pressure cookers will automatically turn off their heat (stovetop pressure cookers must be removed from the heat). Allow the pressure to release from the pot naturally for 10 minutes before releasing the remaining pressure using the manufacturer's quick-release method.

PER SERVING: Calories: 426; Total Fat: 33g; Saturated Fat: 15g; Cholesterol: 265mg; Sodium: 864mg; Carbohydrates: 7g; Fiber: 2g; Protein: 25g

Cinnamon Applesauce

DAIRY-FREE · GLUTEN-FREE · NUT-FREE · VEGAN · MAKES ABOUT 3 CUPS

PREP TIME: 5 minutes

TOTAL COOK TIME: 40 minutes

APPROX. PRESSURE BUILD: 13 minutes

PRESSURE COOK: 6 minutes

PRESSURE RELEASE: 15 to 20 minutes

6 apples, cored and chopped

2 cinnamon sticks

½ cup water

1½ teaspoons fresh lemon juice

½ teaspoon salt

INGREDIENT TIPS

✳ Feel free to use your favorite apple varieties for this applesauce. I prefer a combination of Granny Smith, Honeycrisp, Fuji, and Golden Delicious.

✳ If you don't have whole cinnamon sticks, you can substitute ½ to 1 teaspoon ground cinnamon.

The pressure cooker can make the quickest, most delicious applesauce in the world. However, applesauce is prone to frothing, so it is important to read the safety tips on page 37 before preparing applesauce in your pressure cooker.

1. Put the chopped apples, cinnamon sticks, water, lemon juice, and salt in the pressure cooker pot.

2. Close and lock the pressure cooker lid, make sure the pressure/steam-release switch is set to sealing, and set the cooking time to 6 minutes at high/normal pressure (if using an electric pressure cooker; for stovetop pressure cookers, heat over a burner on high heat, set a timer for 5 minutes after the pot has reached pressure, then reduce the heat to low). It will take 13 minutes for the pot to come to pressure before the cooking time begins (it may be faster for stovetop pressure cookers, so be sure to watch your cooker until you see that the pin has raised completely).

3. After the pressure cooking time ends, electric pressure cookers will automatically turn off their heat (stovetop pressure cookers must be removed from the heat). Allow the pressure to release from the pot naturally, 15 to 20 minutes.

4. Meanwhile, place a colander over a large bowl. When the pressure has released from the pot, tap or lightly shake the pot before removing the lid to pop any trapped steam bubbles that may be below the food's surface. Remove and discard the cinnamon sticks and pour the remaining contents of the pot into the colander.

5. Using a wooden spoon, mash the apples through the holes of the colander. Use tongs to remove and discard the apple peels.

6. If desired, purée the applesauce in a blender. If you like thicker applesauce, there is no need to purée, and you can eat or store the sauce once it has cooled.

PER SERVING (½ CUP): Calories: 116; Total Fat: 0g; Saturated Fat: 0g; Cholesterol: 0mg; Sodium: 196mg; Carbohydrates: 31g; Fiber: 5g; Protein: 1g

SAFETY TIPS

Since applesauce is prone to frothing, it is important to closely monitor the pressure cooking and pressure-release process. When an excess of froth is created, it can block the pressure-release safety valves. Here are some important safety tips for cooking applesauce in a pressure cooker:

* Do not overfill your pot. This recipe was developed for a 6-quart pressure cooker, and it should not be doubled. If using a smaller pressure cooker, reduce the ingredients by half.

* If you see froth or food particles coming out of the pressure-release valve, do not use a quick-release of pressure. Cancel the pressure cooking session (or gently remove the stovetop pressure cooker from its heat source) and let the pressure naturally release from the pot completely before removing the lid.

* Never use quick-release for applesauce or other frothy foods. Always allow the pressure to release from the pot naturally and completely.

* Tap or lightly shake the pot before removing the lid to pop any trapped steam bubbles that may be below the food's surface (otherwise they could pop and cause a food eruption after the lid has been removed).

* Clean all valves on your pressure cooker lid thoroughly after cooking a frothy recipe.

Blueberry Coffee Cake

NUT-FREE • VEGETARIAN • SERVES 8

PREP TIME: 10 minutes	
TOTAL COOK TIME: 1 hour 10 minutes	
APPROX. PRESSURE BUILD: 6 to 7 minutes	
PRESSURE COOK: 35 minutes	
PRESSURE RELEASE: 30 minutes	

Nonstick cooking spray

2¼ cups all-purpose flour, divided

1 teaspoon baking powder

1 teaspoon baking soda

¼ teaspoon salt

1 cup granulated sugar

1 cup plain unsweetened Greek yogurt

8 tablespoons (1 stick) unsalted butter, at room temperature, plus 2 tablespoons, melted

1 large egg

1 cup blueberries

1 cup water

¼ cup brown sugar

¼ teaspoon ground cinnamon

½ cup purchased cream cheese frosting, melted

This is an easy but impressive breakfast to prepare when you have guests. They will never believe that such a moist and fluffy cake was made in a pressure cooker! This recipe uses a 6-cup Bundt pan, which fits into 6- and 8-quart pressure cookers. You might need to use a smaller pan if you have a smaller pressure cooker.

1. Spray a 6-cup Bundt pan with nonstick cooking spray.

2. In a medium bowl, whisk together 2 cups of flour, the baking powder, baking soda, and salt.

3. In a large bowl, beat together the granulated sugar, yogurt, 8 tablespoons room-temperature butter, and egg with a hand mixer until smooth.

4. Add the dry ingredients to the wet ingredients and mix with the hand mixer until completely combined. Fold in the blueberries.

5. Pour the batter into the prepared Bundt pan. Lay a paper towel over the top of the pan (this will help catch excess moisture from the steam inside the pot), then cover the paper towel and pan loosely with aluminum foil.

6. Pour the water into the pressure cooker pot and place a steamer rack trivet in the bottom. Place the foil-covered Bundt pan on the trivet.

COOKING TIP

See the Cooking Tip on page 29 for how to use a bakeware sling.

7. Close and lock the pressure cooker lid, make sure the pressure/steam-release switch is set to sealing, and set the cooking time to 35 minutes at high/normal pressure (if using an electric pressure cooker; for stovetop pressure cookers, heat over a burner on high heat, set a timer for 35 minutes after the pot has reached pressure, then reduce the heat to low). It will take 6 to 7 minutes for the pot to come to pressure before the cooking time begins.

8. After the pressure cooking time ends, electric pressure cookers will automatically turn off their heat (stovetop pressure cookers must be removed from the heat). Allow the pressure to release from the pot naturally, about 30 minutes.

9. Meanwhile, mix the brown sugar, remaining ¼ cup flour, 2 tablespoons melted butter, and cinnamon together in a small bowl until it forms a crumbly texture. Set aside.

10. Carefully remove the Bundt pan from the pot and cool on a wire rack.

11. When cool enough to handle, invert the pan over a serving plate. Drizzle the cake with the melted cream cheese frosting and top with the crumble mixture.

PER SERVING: Calories: 469; Total Fat: 19g; Saturated Fat: 11g; Cholesterol: 63mg; Sodium: 385mg; Carbohydrates: 68g; Fiber: 2g; Protein: 8g

Chocolate Chip Banana Bread

NUT-FREE • VEGETARIAN • SERVES 8

PREP TIME: 10 minutes

TOTAL COOK TIME: 1 hour 20 minutes

APPROX. PRESSURE BUILD: 6 to 7 minutes

PRESSURE COOK: 55 to 60 minutes

PRESSURE RELEASE: 10 minutes

Nonstick cooking spray

¾ cup brown sugar

8 tablespoons (1 stick) unsalted butter, at room temperature

2 large eggs, at room temperature

2 cups mashed overripe bananas (4 to 5 bananas)

2 cups all-purpose flour

1½ teaspoons baking soda

¼ teaspoon salt

¾ cup chocolate chips

1½ cups water

This pressure cooker banana bread recipe is a great way to use up overripe bananas. The addition of chocolate chips make it feel almost like a dessert treat, but I like to eat it for breakfast with a little butter. The recipe uses a 6-cup Bundt pan, which fits into 6- and 8-quart pressure cookers. You might need to use a smaller pan if you have a smaller pressure cooker.

1. Spray a 6-cup Bundt pan with nonstick cooking spray and lightly dust it with flour.

2. In a medium bowl, beat together the brown sugar, butter, and eggs with a hand mixer until creamy. Beat in the mashed bananas until evenly incorporated.

3. Add the flour, baking soda, and salt and beat until well mixed; be careful not to overmix. Fold in the chocolate chips.

4. Pour the batter into the prepared Bundt pan. Lay a paper towel over the top of the pan (this will help catch excess moisture from the steam inside the pot), then cover the paper towel and pan loosely with aluminum foil.

5. Pour the water into the pressure cooker pot and place a steamer rack trivet in the bottom. Place the foil-covered Bundt pan on the trivet.

INGREDIENT TIP

"Baked" goods prepared in the pressure cooker are technically cooked with hot steam instead of hot air as in an oven. As a result, cakes and breads will end up very moist, but with a denser texture. For fluffier "baked" goods in the pressure cooker, and to prevent them from being too dense, be sure to properly measure your flour. Instead of scooping flour out of its container with a measuring cup, spoon the flour into your measuring cup, then gently level it with the back of a knife (as opposed to packing it down).

6. Close and lock the pressure cooker lid, make sure the pressure/steam-release switch is set to sealing, and set the cooking time to 55 minutes at high/normal pressure (if using an electric pressure cooker; for stovetop pressure cookers, heat over a burner on high heat, set a timer for 55 minutes after the pot has reached pressure, then reduce the heat to low). It will take 6 to 7 minutes for the pot to come to pressure before cooking time begins.

7. After the pressure cooking time ends, electric pressure cookers will automatically turn off their heat (stovetop pressure cookers must be removed from the heat). Allow the pressure to release from the pot naturally for 10 minutes before releasing the remaining pressure using the manufacturer's quick-release method.

8. Carefully remove the Bundt pan from the pot. If the bread still seems doughy, replace the paper towel and foil and return it to the pot to pressure cook for an additional 5 minutes.

9. Allow the banana bread to cool completely on a wire rack before removing the bread from the pan.

PER SERVING: Calories: 422; Total Fat: 18g; Saturated Fat: 11g; Cholesterol: 81mg; Sodium: 412mg; Carbohydrates: 60g; Fiber: 3g; Protein: 7g

COOKING TIP
See the Cooking Tip on page 29 for how to use a bakeware sling.

Vanilla Yogurt with Granola and Honey

VEGETARIAN • SERVES 16

PREP TIME: 1 minute

TOTAL COOK TIME: 10 hours 30 minutes

8 cups whole milk

2 tablespoons yogurt with active cultures

4 cups granola, divided

1 cup honey, divided

*One of the most surprising things you can make in an electric pressure cooker is homemade yogurt! Making your own yogurt lets you control the sugar content and customize the flavors and toppings in any way you like. All you need to start is milk and some prepared yogurt with live cultures (*Lactobacillus bulgaricus *and* Streptococcus thermophilus—*check the label to be sure). Note that this recipe is geared for electric multicooker pressure cookers that have a yogurt setting and thus can't be easily adapted for stovetop pressure cookers.*

1. Pour the milk into the inner pot of your pressure cooker and close and lock the lid. It doesn't matter if the pressure/steam-release valve is set to sealing or venting, as this recipe does not cook under pressure. Select the yogurt button and press it a few times until it says "boil." When the boil cycle is complete, open the lid and check the temperature of the milk. It needs to reach a temperature of 180°F, so if it is not yet at that temperature, repeat the boil cycle one or more times until the temperature is reached, then remove the inner pot from your pressure cooker. This will take about 1½ hours.

2. Leave the milk in the pot until it cools to 115°F, about 1 hour.

You'll need a food thermometer to check the temperature of the yogurt at various stages during the cooking process. I suggest using a candy thermometer since you can clip it on the edge of your electric pressure cooker's inner pot when the yogurt is cooling.

3. The milk will have a thin film on the top by the time it has cooled. Gently skim off this layer with a skimmer or slotted spoon and discard.

4. Add the prepared yogurt with active cultures and whisk together until the yogurt is completely blended into the milk.

5. Close and lock the lid. Press the yogurt button until it says "8:00." This will begin an incubation period for the cultures.

6. After 8 hours, the yogurt should be thickened and ready to serve or store in containers in the refrigerator. Serve in ½-cup portions, each topped with ¼ cup granola and 1 tablespoon honey.

PER SERVING: Calories: 316; Total Fat: 9g; Saturated Fat: 6g; Cholesterol: 13mg; Sodium: 72mg; Carbohydrates: 53g; Fiber: 3g; Protein: 8g

SNACKS *and* APPETIZERS

Stuffed Mushrooms

30 MINUTES · GLUTEN-FREE · KETO · NUT-FREE · SERVES 4 TO 6

PREP TIME: 10 minutes

TOTAL COOK TIME:
15 minutes

APPROX. PRESSURE BUILD:
4 minutes

PRESSURE COOK: 6 minutes

PRESSURE RELEASE:
1 minute

1 pound large button
mushrooms (24 to
30 mushrooms)

2 tablespoons
unsalted butter

3 tablespoons finely
chopped onion

3 garlic cloves, minced

8 ounces cream cheese, at
room temperature

¼ cup grated
Parmesan cheese

½ to 1 cup chicken broth,
store-bought or homemade
(page 170)

Coarse salt

Freshly ground
black pepper

*Stuffed mushrooms are a great party appetizer.
You can make a big quantity really quickly, and the
bite-size serving is easy for guests to eat while
they mingle. This pressure cooker version of the
popular appetizer is extra savory since it cooks in
chicken broth.*

1. Remove the stems from the mushrooms and finely
   chop them. Place the mushroom caps upside down on a
   large plate.
2. Select the sauté function on the pressure cooker (if
   using an electric pressure cooker; for stovetop pressure
   cookers, heat over a burner on medium-high heat). Melt
   the butter in the pot.
3. Add the chopped mushroom stems, onion, and garlic
   and sauté for 2 minutes. Press cancel or turn off the
   burner. Pour the vegetable mixture into a medium bowl.
4. Stir the cream cheese and Parmesan cheese into the
   vegetable mixture until well blended.
5. Stuff the mixture into the prepared mushroom caps,
   mounding the filling over the top of the mushrooms.
6. Pour ½ cup of chicken broth into the pressure cooker
   pot and use a wooden spoon to scrape any browned bits
   from the bottom.
7. Using tongs, place the stuffed mushrooms one by one in
   the bottom of the pot so they are sitting in the chicken
   broth. Start by placing them around the edges of the
   pot as they will stay upright easier this way. You may
   need to cook your mushrooms in batches if they cannot
   fit in a single layer in the bottom of the pot.

8. Close and lock the pressure cooker lid, make sure the pressure/steam-release switch is set to sealing, and set the cooking time to 6 minutes at high/normal pressure (if using an electric pressure cooker; for stovetop pressure cookers, heat over a burner on high heat, set a timer for 6 minutes after the pot has reached pressure, then reduce the heat to low). It will take about 4 minutes for the pot to come to pressure before the cooking time begins.

9. After the pressure cooking time ends, electric pressure cookers will automatically turn off their heat (stovetop pressure cookers must be removed from the heat). Release the pressure using the manufacturer's quick-release method.

10. Using tongs, carefully remove the stuffed mushrooms from the pot and transfer to a serving plate. Sprinkle the tops of the mushrooms with coarse salt and freshly ground black pepper.

11. If you are cooking the mushrooms in batches, pour the chicken broth out of the pot and scoop out any melted cheese. Add the remaining ½ cup of chicken broth to the pot and cook the remaining stuffed mushrooms in the same way.

PER SERVING: Calories: 311; Total Fat: 31g; Saturated Fat: 17g; Cholesterol: 89mg; Sodium: 387mg; Carbohydrates: 7g; Fiber: 1g; Protein: 12g

Feta, Spinach, and Artichoke Dip

30 MINUTES • GLUTEN-FREE • KETO • NUT-FREE • VEGETARIAN • SERVES 8

PREP TIME: 5 minutes

TOTAL COOK TIME:
20 minutes

APPROX. PRESSURE BUILD:
7 to 8 minutes

PRESSURE COOK: 12 minutes

PRESSURE RELEASE:
1 minute

1½ cups water

1 cup mayonnaise

½ cup grated
Parmesan cheese

4 ounces feta cheese,
crumbled

1 (14-ounce) can
artichoke hearts, drained
and chopped

1 (10-ounce) package
frozen chopped spinach,
thawed and drained

2 garlic cloves, minced

¼ teaspoon freshly ground
black pepper

This quick pot-in-pot dip recipe comes out so perfect that you'll never make spinach and artichoke dip in your slow cooker or oven again. The feta cheese adds a light bite that sets this recipe apart from other spinach and artichoke dips. You can serve the dip with chunks of French bread, tortilla strips, or even vegetables if you want to keep this recipe keto-friendly.

1. Pour the water into the pressure cooker pot and place a steamer rack trivet in the bottom.

2. In a heat-safe bowl (I use a 7-cup glass bowl), mix the mayonnaise, Parmesan cheese, feta cheese, artichoke hearts, spinach, garlic, and pepper.

3. Cover the bowl with aluminum foil and place it on the trivet inside the pot.

4. Close and lock the pressure cooker lid, make sure the pressure/steam-release switch is set to sealing, and set the cooking time to 12 minutes at high/normal pressure (if using an electric pressure cooker; for stovetop pressure cookers, heat over a burner on high heat, set a timer for 12 minutes after the pot has reached pressure, then reduce the heat to low). It will take 7 to 8 minutes for the pot to come to pressure with an electric pressure cooker (stovetop pressure cookers may reach pressure sooner).

5. After the pressure cooking time ends, electric pressure cookers will automatically turn off their heat (stovetop pressure cookers must be removed from the heat). Release the pressure using the manufacturer's quick-release method.

6. Remove the bowl from the pressure cooker and stir the dip before serving.

PER SERVING: Calories: 273; Total Fat: 25g; Saturated Fat: 6g; Cholesterol: 28mg; Sodium: 478mg; Carbohydrates: 8g; Fiber: 4g; Protein: 7g

Pepperoni Pizza Dip

30 MINUTES • GLUTEN-FREE • NUT-FREE • SERVES 6

PREP TIME: 5 minutes

TOTAL COOK TIME:
25 minutes

APPROX. PRESSURE BUILD:
8 to 9 minutes

PRESSURE COOK: 15 minutes

PRESSURE RELEASE:
1 minute

1½ cups water

8 ounces cream cheese, at room temperature

2 cups shredded mozzarella cheese, divided

½ teaspoon garlic powder

¼ teaspoon freshly ground black pepper

1 cup pizza sauce

⅓ cup mini pepperoni

½ teaspoon dried oregano

INGREDIENT TIP

If you don't have mini pepperoni, you can chop regular-size pepperoni pieces into quarters to make them bite-size.

My family fights over the last bites of this delicious layered appetizer dip. It is also a hit at parties. Kids love it because it tastes exactly like pizza. Adults love it because it's low in carbs but satisfies that pizza craving. Serve with tortilla strips, garlic pita chips, or Melba toast, or try low-carb veggie dippers.

1. Pour the water into the pressure cooker pot and place a steamer rack trivet in the bottom.
2. In a small bowl, mix together the cream cheese, 1 cup of mozzarella cheese, garlic powder, and pepper. Spread the cream cheese mixture into the bottom of a heat-safe bowl (I use a 7-cup glass bowl).
3. Spread the pizza sauce over the cream cheese mixture, then top with the remaining 1 cup of mozzarella cheese. Scatter the mini pepperoni evenly on the top of the cheese, then sprinkle with the oregano.
4. Cover the bowl with aluminum foil and place it on the trivet inside the pot.

COOKING TIP

See the Cooking Tip on page 29 for how to use a bakeware sling.

5. Close and lock the pressure cooker lid, make sure the pressure/steam-release switch is set to sealing, and set the cooking time to 15 minutes at high/normal pressure (if using an electric pressure cooker; for stovetop pressure cookers, heat over a burner on high heat, set a timer for 15 minutes after the pot has reached pressure, then reduce the heat to low). It will take 7 to 8 minutes for the pot to come to pressure with an electric pressure cooker (stovetop pressure cookers may reach pressure sooner).

6. After the pressure cooking time ends, electric pressure cookers will automatically turn off their heat (stovetop pressure cookers must be removed from the heat). Release the pressure using the manufacturer's quick-release method.

7. Remove the bowl from the pressure cooker and serve immediately.

PER SERVING: Calories: 291; Total Fat: 24g; Saturated Fat: 14g; Cholesterol: 74mg; Sodium: 547mg; Carbohydrates: 8g; Fiber: 2g; Protein: 12g

Tex-Mex Queso

30 MINUTES • GLUTEN-FREE • NUT-FREE • SERVES 8

PREP TIME: 5 minutes
TOTAL COOK TIME: 25 minutes
APPROX. PRESSURE BUILD: 9 to 10 minutes
PRESSURE COOK: 4 minutes
PRESSURE RELEASE: 1 minute

1 pound ground turkey

¼ teaspoon salt

⅛ teaspoon freshly ground black pepper

⅛ teaspoon garlic powder

1 (10-ounce) can diced tomatoes with green chiles (such as Ro-Tel)

1 (32-ounce) block easy-melt cheese (such as Velveeta), cut into 1-inch chunks

2 tablespoons chopped fresh cilantro

Adapted from my Texan husband's slow-cooker queso recipe, this pressure cooker version is done and ready to serve in a fraction of the time. We serve it with tortilla strips or chips, but it can also be used as a sauce or dip for low-carb vegetables, such as celery, cauliflower, and green bell pepper.

1. Select the sauté function on the pressure cooker (if using an electric pressure cooker; for stovetop pressure cookers, heat over a burner on medium-high heat). Once the pot is hot, add the ground turkey, salt, pepper, and garlic powder and cook, stirring frequently, until the turkey is browned and cooked through, about 8 minutes.

2. Press cancel or turn off the burner. Stir in the diced tomatoes with green chiles, along with their juices.

3. Lay the chunks of easy-melt cheese evenly over the top of the meat and tomatoes.

4. Close and lock the pressure cooker lid, make sure the pressure/steam-release switch is set to sealing, and set the cooking time to 4 minutes at high/normal pressure (if using an electric pressure cooker; for stovetop pressure cookers, heat over a burner on high heat, set a timer for 3 minutes after the pot has reached pressure, then reduce the heat to low). It will take 9 to 10 minutes for the pot to come to pressure before the cooking time begins.

For some extra spice, you can add taco seasoning to the meat while it's browning and choose a hotter version of the diced tomatoes with green chiles.

5. After the pressure cooking time ends, electric pressure cookers will automatically turn off their heat (stovetop pressure cookers must be removed from the heat). Release the pressure using the manufacturer's quick release method.

6. Stir in the cilantro and transfer the queso to a serving bowl.

PER SERVING: Calories: 388; Total Fat: 25g; Saturated Fat: 14g; Cholesterol: 111mg; Sodium: 1845mg; Carbohydrates: 13g; Fiber: 0g; Protein: 34g

SERVING TIP

Serve this with low-carb vegetables, such as celery, cauliflower, and green bell pepper, instead of tortilla chips for a lower-carb alternative.

Garlic-Sesame Chicken Wings

30 MINUTES • DAIRY-FREE • NUT-FREE • SERVES 8

PREP TIME: 5 minutes

TOTAL COOK TIME:
25 minutes

APPROX. PRESSURE BUILD:
6 minutes

PRESSURE COOK: 5 minutes

PRESSURE RELEASE:
10 minutes

3 pounds chicken wings

Salt

Freshly ground
black pepper

2 tablespoons toasted
sesame oil

4 garlic cloves, minced

¼ cup soy sauce

¼ cup hoisin sauce

1 tablespoon honey

¼ cup plus 1 tablespoon
water, divided

1 tablespoon cornstarch

2 tablespoons chopped
scallions (green parts only)

1 tablespoon toasted
sesame seeds

I've always been a fan of garlicky wing sauce, so I love to serve this option alongside traditional Buffalo-style chicken wings for game-watching parties. Pressure cooking infuses these savory wings with serious flavor, and you can customize the thickness and stickiness of the sauce to your preference by increasing the cornstarch.

1. Season the chicken wings with salt and pepper.

2. Select the sauté function on the pressure cooker (if using an electric pressure cooker; for stovetop pressure cookers, heat over a burner on medium-high heat). Heat the sesame oil in the pot.

3. Add the chicken wings and garlic to the pot and sauté until the wings are browned, about 2 minutes per side. Press cancel or turn off the burner. Remove the chicken from the pot and set aside.

4. In a medium bowl, whisk together the soy sauce, hoisin sauce, and honey until smooth.

5. Pour ¼ cup of water into the pressure cooker pot and use a wooden spoon to scrape any browned bits from the bottom.

6. Return the chicken wings to the pot and pour the soy sauce mixture over them.

7. Close and lock the pressure cooker lid, make sure the pressure/steam-release switch is set to sealing, and set the cooking time to 5 minutes at high/normal pressure (if using an electric pressure cooker; for stovetop pressure cookers, heat over a burner on high heat, set a timer for 5 minutes after the pot has reached pressure, then reduce the heat to low). It will take about 6 minutes

For an extra thick and sticky sauce, make your slurry with 2 tablespoons of cornstarch and 2 tablespoons water, and stir an additional 1 tablespoon of honey into the sauce at the end.

for the pot to come to pressure before the cooking time begins.

8. After the pressure cooking time ends, electric pressure cookers will automatically turn off their heat (stovetop pressure cookers must be removed from the heat). Allow the pressure to release from the pot naturally for 10 minutes before releasing the remaining pressure using the manufacturer's quick-release method.

9. Open the lid and remove the chicken with tongs or a slotted spoon and set aside in a bowl.

10. In a small bowl, whisk together the cornstarch and remaining 1 tablespoon of water to make a slurry.

11. Select the sauté function on the pot again and whisk the slurry into the sauce. Simmer until the sauce thickens, about 2 minutes, then press cancel or turn off the burner.

12. Return the chicken wings to the pot, along with the scallions and sesame seeds, and toss together with the sauce. Transfer to a serving dish.

PER SERVING: Calories: 448; Total Fat: 31g; Saturated Fat: 8g; Cholesterol: 128mg; Sodium: 726mg; Carbohydrates: 8g; Fiber: 1g; Protein: 33g

INGREDIENT TIP

You can use chicken wing "flats" or drumettes, or a combination of both, for this recipe.

Cola and Brown Sugar Sausage Bites

DAIRY-FREE · GLUTEN-FREE · NUT-FREE · SERVES 8 TO 10

PREP TIME: 5 minutes	
TOTAL COOK TIME: 30 minutes	
APPROX. PRESSURE BUILD: 11 to 12 minutes	
PRESSURE COOK: 5 minutes	
PRESSURE RELEASE: 10 minutes	

1 (12-ounce) can cola

¼ cup ketchup

2 tablespoons brown sugar

½ teaspoon freshly ground black pepper

½ teaspoon garlic powder

¼ teaspoon onion powder

1 (24-ounce) package mini smoked sausages (such as Lit'l Smokies)

The lightly spicy-sweet flavor of cola pairs really well with the caramel notes of brown sugar. The two work together to make delicious ham glazes and barbecue sauces. In this sweet and savory sausage appetizer, I've brought the two flavors together with ketchup and spices in a recipe that will be ready for your tailgate or game-watching party in just over 30 minutes.

1. Pour the can of cola into the pressure cooker pot, then stir in the ketchup, brown sugar, pepper, garlic powder, and onion powder until well blended.
2. Add the smoked sausages and stir until they are coated with the sauce.
3. Close and lock the pressure cooker lid, make sure the pressure/steam-release switch is set to sealing, and set the cooking time to 5 minutes at high/normal pressure (if using an electric pressure cooker; for stovetop pressure cookers, heat over a burner on high heat, set a timer for 5 minutes after the pot has reached pressure, then reduce the heat to low). It will take 11 to 12 minutes for the pot to come to pressure before the cooking time begins.

4. After the pressure cooking time ends, electric pressure cookers will automatically turn off their heat (stovetop pressure cookers must be removed from the heat). Allow the pressure to release from the pot naturally for 10 minutes before releasing the remaining pressure using the manufacturer's quick-release method.
5. Open the lid and stir the contents of the pot.
6. Select the sauté function on the pot (if using an electric pressure cooker; for stovetop pressure cookers, heat over a burner on medium-high heat). Simmer for 5 minutes, stirring occasionally, so the sauce can reduce and thicken slightly. Press cancel or turn off the burner. Transfer the sausages and sauce to a serving dish and serve with toothpicks.

PER SERVING: Calories: 297; Total Fat: 24g; Saturated Fat: 8g; Cholesterol: 51mg; Sodium: 783mg; Carbohydrates: 10g; Fiber: 0g; Protein: 10g

INGREDIENT TIP

If you don't have mini smoked sausages, you can make this with 2 (14-ounce) packages of full-size smoked sausages, sliced about ½ inch thick.

Teriyaki Pineapple Meatballs

30 MINUTES · DAIRY-FREE · NUT-FREE · MAKES 14 MEATBALLS

PREP TIME: 10 minutes

TOTAL COOK TIME:
30 minutes

APPROX. PRESSURE BUILD:
7 to 8 minutes

PRESSURE COOK: 7 minutes

PRESSURE RELEASE:
5 minutes

8 ounces ground pork

8 ounces ground turkey

½ cup bread crumbs

¼ cup minced onion

1 large egg, lightly beaten

½ teaspoon garlic powder

½ teaspoon salt

¼ teaspoon freshly ground
black pepper

1 tablespoon vegetable oil

1 (20-ounce) can pineapple
chunks, drained and juice
reserved

½ cup teriyaki sauce

2 tablespoons soy sauce

1 red bell pepper, seeded
and coarsely chopped

1 tablespoon cornstarch

1 tablespoon water

*The lightly tropical flavor makes these meatballs a
great hors d'oeuvre choice to serve at a summer party.
They can also double as a main dish when served
over steamed rice.*

1. In a medium bowl, mix together the ground pork,
    ground turkey, bread crumbs, onion, egg, garlic powder,
    salt, and pepper. Using your hands, form the mixture
    into 2-inch meatballs.

2. Select the sauté function on the pressure cooker (if
    using an electric pressure cooker; for stovetop pressure
    cookers, heat over a burner on medium-high heat). Heat
    the vegetable oil in the pot.

3. Add the meatballs to the pot and cook until browned
    on all sides, 6 to 8 minutes. Press cancel or turn off the
    burner. Using tongs, transfer the meatballs to a plate
    and set aside.

4. In a medium bowl, whisk together the reserved pine-
    apple juice, teriyaki sauce, and soy sauce.

5. Pour the sauce into the pressure cooker pot and use
    a wooden spoon to scrape any browned bits from
    the bottom.

6. Return the meatballs to the pot, along with the pine-
    apple chunks and bell pepper.

I recommend using a thicker teriyaki glaze sauce as opposed to the thinner teriyaki marinade that is more like soy sauce in consistency.

7. Close and lock the pressure cooker lid, make sure the pressure/steam-release switch is set to sealing, and set the cooking time to 7 minutes at high/normal pressure (if using an electric pressure cooker; for stovetop pressure cookers, heat over a burner on high heat, set a timer for 7 minutes after the pot has reached pressure, then reduce the heat to low). It will take 7 to 8 minutes for the pot to come to pressure before the cooking time begins.

8. After the pressure cooking time ends, electric pressure cookers will automatically turn off their heat (stovetop pressure cookers must be removed from the heat). Allow the pressure to release from the pot naturally for 5 minutes before releasing the remaining pressure using the manufacturer's quick-release method.

9. In a small bowl, whisk together the cornstarch and water to make a slurry.

10. Open the lid, select the sauté function on the pot again, and whisk the slurry into the sauce. Simmer until the sauce thickens, about 2 minutes, then press cancel or turn off the burner.

11. Transfer the meatballs and sauce to a serving dish and serve with toothpicks.

PER SERVING (1 MEATBALL): Calories: 127; Total Fat: 6g; Saturated Fat: 2g; Cholesterol: 38mg; Sodium: 664mg; Carbohydrates: 11g; Fiber: 1g; Protein: 8g

Texas Sushi (Spicy Bacon-Wrapped Steak Bites)

GLUTEN-FREE · NUT-FREE · SERVES 6

PREP TIME: 10 minutes	
TOTAL COOK TIME: 20 minutes	
APPROX. PRESSURE BUILD: 7 minutes	
PRESSURE COOK: 10 minutes	
PRESSURE RELEASE: 1 minute	

1 cup beef broth

6 (2-inch) chunks beef stew meat (about 1½ pounds total)

Salt

Freshly ground black pepper

Garlic powder

2 jalapeño peppers, seeded and cut into 6 (1- to 2-inch) chunks

1 green bell pepper, seeded and cut into 6 (2-inch) chunks

6 (2-inch) chunks onion

6 bacon strips

3 ounces cream cheese (from a block), cut into 2-by-1-by-½-inch slices

In Texas we love steak, bacon, and jalapeño peppers. This low-carb appetizer is a little bit of all of that and is great to serve for a party when you don't have access to a grill.

1. Pour the beef broth into the pressure cooker pot and place a steamer rack trivet in the bottom.
2. Season the beef chunks with salt, pepper, and garlic powder.
3. On top of each beef chunk, layer a chunk of jalapeño pepper, bell pepper, and onion.
4. Wrap a strip of bacon around each stack of beef and vegetables and secure it with a toothpick. Place the bundles in a single layer on the trivet inside the pot.
5. Close and lock the pressure cooker lid, make sure the pressure/steam-release switch is set to sealing, and set the cooking time to 10 minutes at high/normal pressure (if using an electric pressure cooker; for stovetop pressure cookers, heat over a burner on high heat, set a timer for 10 minutes after the pot has reached pressure, then reduce the heat to low). It will take about 7 minutes for the pot to come to pressure with an electric pressure cooker (stovetop pressure cookers may reach pressure sooner).
6. After the pressure cooking time ends, electric pressure cookers will automatically turn off their heat (stovetop pressure cookers must be removed from the heat). Release the pressure using the manufacturer's quick-release method.

7. Open the lid and carefully remove each bundle with tongs and set on a plate. Remove the trivet, discard the broth, and wipe out the pressure cooker pot.

8. One at a time, carefully unwrap the bacon from each bundle and add a slice of cream cheese between the beef and jalapeño. Rewrap the bacon around the bundle and secure it with the toothpick again.

9. Select the sauté function on the pressure cooker (if using an electric pressure cooker; for stovetop pressure cookers, heat over a burner on medium-high heat). Using tongs, place the bundles in the pot to brown for about 4 minutes on one side; then flip and brown for 4 minutes on the opposite side. Press cancel or turn off the burner. Using tongs, remove the bundles from the pot and serve.

PER SERVING: Calories: 302; Total Fat: 17g; Saturated Fat: 6g; Cholesterol: 36mg; Sodium: 606mg; Carbohydrates: 16g; Fiber: 4g; Protein: 23g

5

VEGETABLES and SIDES

63

Herbed Asparagus

30 MINUTES • DAIRY-FREE • GLUTEN-FREE • NUT-FREE • VEGAN • SERVES 4 TO 6

PREP TIME: 5 minutes

TOTAL COOK TIME:
10 minutes

APPROX. PRESSURE BUILD:
4 to 5 minutes

PRESSURE COOK: 1 minute

PRESSURE RELEASE:
1 minute

1 cup water

1 pound asparagus spears, woody ends snapped off

Olive oil

¼ teaspoon dried basil

¼ teaspoon dried rosemary

¼ teaspoon dried thyme

Coarse salt

Freshly ground black pepper

COOKING TIP

If you like your asparagus crisper, try this: Close and lock the pressure cooker lid, make sure the pressure/steam-release switch is set to sealing, and set the cooking time to 0 minutes at high/normal pressure (if using an electric pressure cooker; for stovetop pressure cookers, heat over a burner on high heat, then remove the pressure cooker from the heat as soon as the pot reaches pressure).

This zesty side dish can be customized with any of your favorite herbs and spices. Or, leave out the oil and herbs and try a squeeze of fresh lemon juice over the asparagus as an alternative.

1. Pour the water into the pressure cooker pot and place a steamer rack trivet in the bottom.

2. Arrange the asparagus in a steamer basket and drizzle with olive oil. Sprinkle with the basil, rosemary, and thyme and season with salt and pepper. Place the steamer basket on the trivet in the pressure cooker.

3. Close and lock the pressure cooker lid, make sure the pressure/steam-release switch is set to sealing, and set the cooking time to 1 minute at high/normal pressure (if using an electric pressure cooker; for stovetop pressure cookers, heat over a burner on high heat, set a timer for 1 minute after the pot has reached pressure, then reduce the heat to low). It will take 4 to 5 minutes for the pot to come to pressure before the cooking time begins.

4. After the pressure cooking time ends, electric pressure cookers will automatically turn off their heat (stovetop pressure cookers must be removed from the heat). Release the pressure using the manufacturer's quick-release method.

PER SERVING: Calories: 53; Total Fat: 4g; Saturated Fat: 1g; Cholesterol: 0mg; Sodium: 76mg; Carbohydrates: 5g; Fiber: 2g; Protein: 3g

Steamed Artichokes

30 MINUTES · DAIRY-FREE · GLUTEN-FREE · NUT-FREE · VEGAN · SERVES 2 TO 4

PREP TIME: 1 minute
TOTAL COOK TIME: 25 minutes
APPROX. PRESSURE BUILD: 4 to 5 minutes
PRESSURE COOK: 20 minutes
PRESSURE RELEASE: 1 minute

1 cup water

2 to 4 artichokes, tops and stems trimmed

1 to 2 lemons

Garlic salt

SERVING TIP

Artichoke leaves are delicious with mayonnaise and yogurt-based dipping sauces, especially ones with garlic and lemon. You can also dip the leaves in butter, vinaigrette, or a mustard sauce. With all of these sauce choices, it's unlikely you'll get bored with this superfood vegetable anytime soon.

Artichokes are one of the most antioxidant-rich vegetables, low in fat, and loaded with vitamins and minerals. If you don't make whole artichokes often enough, the pressure cooker may change that. This easy, hands-off recipe makes it simple to prepare perfectly steamed artichokes.

1. Pour the water into the pressure cooker pot and place a steamer rack trivet in the bottom.
2. Arrange the artichokes standing up on the trivet in the pressure cooker.
3. Squeeze the juice from half of a lemon over each artichoke, then sprinkle with garlic salt (trying to get some of the seasoning under the leaves).
4. Close and lock the pressure cooker lid, make sure the pressure/steam-release switch is set to sealing, and set the cooking time to 20 minutes at high/normal pressure (if using an electric pressure cooker; for stovetop pressure cookers, heat over a burner on high heat, set a timer for 20 minutes after the pot has reached pressure, then reduce the heat to low). It will take 4 to 5 minutes for the pot to come to pressure before the cooking time begins.
5. After the pressure cooking time ends, electric pressure cookers will automatically turn off their heat (stovetop pressure cookers must be removed from the heat). Release the pressure using the manufacturer's quick-release method.

PER SERVING: Calories: 76; Total Fat: 0g; Saturated Fat: 0g; Cholesterol: 0mg; Sodium: 152mg; Carbohydrates: 17g; Fiber: 9g; Protein: 5g

Broccoli with Garlic and Lemon

30 MINUTES • GLUTEN-FREE • KETO • NUT-FREE • VEGETARIAN • SERVES 4

PREP TIME: 5 minutes

TOTAL COOK TIME:
10 minutes

APPROX. PRESSURE BUILD:
4 to 8 minutes

PRESSURE COOK: 1 minute

PRESSURE RELEASE:
1 minute

½ cup water

1 broccoli head, chopped
into florets

1 lemon, cut into 6 wedges

2 tablespoons
unsalted butter, cold,
coarsely chopped

2 garlic cloves,
finely chopped

Coarse salt

Freshly ground
black pepper

This 10-minute vegetable side dish is a dream for garlic lovers. If you don't like garlic, lemon, or butter, you can make this recipe without any of them. Simply prepare the broccoli plain (or feel free to customize your seasonings) and use the same cooking time.

1. Pour the water into the pressure cooker pot and place a steamer rack trivet in the bottom.
2. Put the broccoli florets in a steamer basket. Scatter the lemon wedges, chopped butter, and garlic over the broccoli. Season with salt and pepper. Place the steamer basket on the trivet in the pressure cooker.
3. Close and lock the pressure cooker lid, make sure the pressure/steam-release switch is set to sealing, and set the cooking time to 1 minute at high/normal pressure (if using an electric pressure cooker; for stovetop pressure cookers, heat over a burner on high heat, set a timer for 1 minute after the pot has reached pressure, then reduce the heat to low). It will take 4 minutes for the pot to come to pressure with an electric pressure cooker and 7 to 8 minutes to come to pressure with a stovetop pressure cooker before the cooking time begins.

4. After the pressure cooking time ends, electric pressure cookers will automatically turn off their heat (stovetop pressure cookers must be removed from the heat). Release the pressure using the manufacturer's quick-release method.

5. Remove the steamer basket from the pot. Squeeze 3 lemon wedges over the broccoli and discard the remaining lemon wedges.

PER SERVING: Calories: 88; Total Fat: 6g; Saturated Fat: 4g; Cholesterol: 15mg; Sodium: 145mg; Carbohydrates: 8g; Fiber: 3g; Protein: 3g

COOKING TIP

If you like your broccoli crisper, try this: Close and lock the pressure cooker lid, make sure the pressure/steam-release switch is set to sealing, and set the cooking time to 0 minutes at high/normal pressure (if using an electric pressure cooker; for stovetop pressure cookers, heat over a burner on high heat, then remove the pressure cooker from the heat as soon as the pot reaches pressure).

Perfect Corn on the Cob

30 MINUTES · GLUTEN-FREE · NUT-FREE · VEGETARIAN · SERVES 4

PREP TIME: 1 minute

TOTAL COOK TIME:
10 minutes

APPROX. PRESSURE BUILD:
4 to 8 minutes

PRESSURE COOK: 2 minutes

PRESSURE RELEASE:
1 minute

1 cup water

4 ears corn, husks and
silk removed

4 tablespoons (½ stick)
unsalted butter, at room
temperature

Salt

Pressure-cooked corn always comes out crisp and moist. Since none of the flavor is boiled off or lost in escaping steam, your corn will taste naturally sweet and buttery. This recipe was written for 4 ears of corn, but you can cook from 1 to 12 ears at the same time with the same instructions. With more than 6 ears, you may have to arrange your corn standing straight up on the trivet (as opposed to laying it flat on the trivet).

1. Pour the water into the pressure cooker pot and place a steamer rack trivet in the bottom.
2. Arrange the corn on top of the trivet (it is okay if the ears overlap or stack).
3. Close and lock the pressure cooker lid, make sure the pressure/steam-release switch is set to sealing, and set the cooking time to 2 minutes at high/normal pressure (if using an electric pressure cooker; for stovetop pressure cookers, heat over a burner on high heat, set a timer for 2 minutes after the pot has reached pressure, then reduce the heat to low). It will take 7 to 8 minutes for the pot to come to pressure with an electric pressure cooker and 4 minutes to come to pressure with a stovetop pressure cooker before the cooking time begins.

4. After the pressure cooking time ends, electric pressure cookers will automatically turn off their heat (stovetop pressure cookers must be removed from the heat). Release the pressure using the manufacturer's quick-release method.

5. Serve with butter and salt.

PER SERVING: Calories: 242; Total Fat: 12g; Saturated Fat: 7g; Cholesterol: 31mg; Sodium: 249mg; Carbohydrates: 34g; Fiber: 2g; Protein: 5g

INGREDIENT TIP

If your ears of corn are too long, you can trim them or cut them in half so that they will fit in the pot more easily.

Spaghetti Squash

30 MINUTES • DAIRY-FREE • GLUTEN-FREE • NUT-FREE • VEGAN • SERVES 8

PREP TIME: 1 minute

TOTAL COOK TIME:
20 minutes

APPROX. PRESSURE BUILD:
7 minutes

PRESSURE COOK: 7 minutes

PRESSURE RELEASE:
5 minutes

1 cup water

1 spaghetti squash

Spaghetti squash is a fabulous lower-carb alternative to pasta. I have found that it can easily stand in for spaghetti, linguine, fettucine, or angel hair if topped with sauce. When prepared in the oven, spaghetti squash can take up to an hour to cook. In the pressure cooker, it's done in 20 minutes.

1. Pour the water into the pressure cooker pot and place a steamer rack trivet in the bottom.
2. Cut the spaghetti squash in half lengthwise and scoop out the seeds with a spoon. Discard the seeds.
3. Arrange the two halves of the squash, cut-side up, on top of the trivet in the pressure cooker (it is okay if they overlap a bit).
4. Close and lock the pressure cooker lid, make sure the pressure/steam-release switch is set to sealing, and set the cooking time to 7 minutes at high/normal pressure (if using an electric pressure cooker; for stovetop pressure cookers, heat over a burner on high heat, set a timer for 7 minutes after the pot has reached pressure, then reduce the heat to low). It will take about 7 minutes for the pot to come to pressure before the cooking time begins.

5. After the pressure cooking time ends, electric pressure cookers will automatically turn off their heat (stovetop pressure cookers must be removed from the heat). Allow the pressure to release from the pot naturally for 5 minutes before releasing the remaining pressure using the manufacturer's quick-release method.

6. Remove the spaghetti squash halves from the pot. Using an oven mitt to hold the squash steady, scrape a fork horizontally across the cut side to loosen the spaghetti-like strands.

PER SERVING: Calories: 35; Total Fat: 1g; Saturated Fat: 0g; Cholesterol: 0mg; Sodium: 19mg; Carbohydrates: 8g; Fiber: 0g; Protein: 1g

Ranch Brussels Sprouts, Carrots, and Red Potatoes

30 MINUTES • GLUTEN-FREE • NUT-FREE • SERVES 6 TO 8

PREP TIME: 10 minutes

TOTAL COOK TIME:
25 minutes

APPROX. PRESSURE BUILD:
10 minutes plus 5 to 6 more minutes

PRESSURE COOK: 7 minutes

PRESSURE RELEASE:
1 minute

1 cup chicken broth, store-bought or homemade (page 170)

2 pounds red potatoes, cut into 1½-inch pieces

3 tablespoons powdered ranch seasoning mix (one 1-ounce packet), divided

1 pound Brussels sprouts, trimmed

4 carrots, peeled and cut into 1½-inch pieces

Zesty ranch seasoning mix takes otherwise plain vegetables up a notch in this hearty side dish. It comes to pressure in two different phases to cook the vegetables evenly. Serve it with pork chops, pork roast, beef stew, or corned beef for a delicious meal.

1. Pour the chicken broth into the pressure cooker pot, then add the red potatoes. Season the potatoes with 2 tablespoons of ranch seasoning mix.

2. Close and lock the pressure cooker lid, make sure the pressure/steam-release switch is set to sealing, and set the cooking time to 4 minutes at high/normal pressure (if using an electric pressure cooker; for stovetop pressure cookers, heat over a burner on high heat, set a timer for 4 minutes after the pot has reached pressure, then reduce the heat to low). It will take about 10 minutes for the pot to come to pressure before the cooking time begins.

3. After the pressure cooking time ends, release the pressure using the manufacturer's quick-release method.

4. Open the lid and add the Brussels sprouts and carrots to the pot. Sprinkle with the remaining 1 tablespoon of ranch seasoning mix.

5. Close, lock, and seal the lid again and set the cooking time to 3 minutes at high/normal pressure (if using an electric pressure cooker; for stovetop pressure cookers, heat over a burner on high heat once more, set a timer for 3 minutes after the pot has reached pressure, then reduce the heat to low). It will take 5 to 6 minutes for the pot to reach pressure the second time.

6. After the pressure cooking time ends, electric pressure cookers will automatically turn off their heat (stovetop pressure cookers must be removed from the heat). Release the pressure using the manufacturer's quick-release method again.

7. Open the lid and stir the vegetables before serving.

PER SERVING: Calories: 168; Total Fat: 3g; Saturated Fat: 0g; Cholesterol: 4mg; Sodium: 438mg; Carbohydrates: 35g; Fiber: 6g; Protein: 7g

Sweet Jalapeño Cornbread

GLUTEN-FREE • NUT-FREE • VEGETARIAN • SERVES 6

PREP TIME: 5 minutes	
TOTAL COOK TIME: 1 hour 10 minutes	
APPROX. PRESSURE BUILD: 6 minutes	
PRESSURE COOK: 1 hour	
PRESSURE RELEASE: 1 minute	

1 cup cornmeal

1 cup all-purpose flour, sifted

½ cup sugar

4 teaspoons baking powder

½ teaspoon salt

1 cup milk

¼ cup shortening, softened

1 large egg

1 jalapeño pepper, seeded and finely chopped

1 cup water

This Texas-style cornbread is not as spicy as it might sound. If the idea of jalapeño peppers doesn't appeal to you, the recipe will still turn out delicious without them. On the other hand, if you really like heat, you can add more chopped jalapeño.

1. In a medium bowl, whisk together the cornmeal, flour, sugar, baking powder, and salt.

2. Slowly add the milk, shortening, and egg, whisking until the batter is smooth. Stir in the chopped jalapeño pepper.

3. Pour the batter into a heat-safe bowl (I use a 7-cup glass bowl) and spread out evenly. Lay a paper towel over the top of the bowl (this will help catch excess moisture from the steam inside the pot), then cover the paper towel and bowl with aluminum foil.

4. Pour the water into the pressure cooker pot and place a steamer rack trivet in the bottom. Place the foil-covered bowl on the trivet.

5. Close and lock the pressure cooker lid, make sure the pressure/steam-release switch is set to sealing, and set the cooking time to 1 hour at high/normal pressure (if using an electric pressure cooker; for stovetop pressure cookers, heat over a burner on high heat, set a timer for 1 hour after the pot has reached pressure, then reduce the heat to low). It will take 6 minutes for the pot to come to pressure before the cooking time begins.

6. After the pressure cooking time ends, electric pressure cookers will automatically turn off their heat (stovetop pressure cookers must be removed from the heat). Release the pressure using the manufacturer's quick-release method.

7. Carefully remove the bowl from the pot and stick a toothpick in the center of the bread to test doneness. If your toothpick comes out clean, the cornbread is done. If not, replace the paper towel and foil and return the bowl to pressure cook for an additional 5 minutes.

8. Cool the cornbread in the bowl on a wire rack. You can either slice and serve it directly from the bowl or remove the bread from the bowl and transfer to a serving dish.

PER SERVING: Calories: 324; Total Fat: 11g; Saturated Fat: 4g; Cholesterol: 34mg; Sodium: 235mg; Carbohydrates: 52g; Fiber: 2g; Protein: 6g

COOKING TIP

See the Cooking Tip on page 29 for how to use a bakeware sling.

Garlic-Parmesan Fingerling Potatoes

30 MINUTES · GLUTEN-FREE · NUT-FREE · VEGETARIAN · SERVES 4 TO 6

PREP TIME: 5 minutes

TOTAL COOK TIME:
20 minutes

APPROX. PRESSURE BUILD:
4 minutes

PRESSURE COOK: 15 minutes

PRESSURE RELEASE:
1 minute

1 cup water

1½ pounds fingerling
potatoes

Olive oil

1 tablespoon minced garlic

1½ teaspoons dried parsley

Coarse salt

Freshly ground
black pepper

3 tablespoons grated
Parmesan cheese

If you're looking for a new way to serve potatoes, this impressive side dish will be on your table in fewer than 30 minutes. Not a big garlic lover? You can reduce the amount of garlic in the recipe to your preference.

1. Pour the water into the pressure cooker pot and place a steamer rack trivet in the bottom.

2. Arrange the potatoes in a steamer basket and drizzle with olive oil. Top with the garlic and parsley, then season with salt and pepper. Place the steamer basket on the trivet in the pressure cooker.

3. Close and lock the pressure cooker lid, make sure the pressure/steam-release switch is set to sealing, and set the cooking time to 15 minutes at high/normal pressure (if using an electric pressure cooker; for stovetop pressure cookers, heat over a burner on high heat, set a timer for 15 minutes after the pot has reached pressure, then reduce the heat to low). It will take about 4 minutes for the pot to come to pressure before the cooking time begins.

4. After the pressure cooking time ends, electric pressure cookers will automatically turn off their heat (stovetop pressure cookers must be removed from the heat). Release the pressure using the manufacturer's quick-release method.

5. Remove the steamer basket from the pot and transfer the potatoes to a serving bowl. Toss with the Parmesan cheese.

PER SERVING: Calories: 155; Total Fat: 3g; Saturated Fat: 1g; Cholesterol: 5mg; Sodium: 149mg; Carbohydrates: 28g; Fiber: 3g; Protein: 6g

INGREDIENT TIP

If you can't find fingerling potatoes, you can easily substitute new potatoes or small red or Yukon Gold potatoes in this recipe.

6

SEAFOOD

Mussels in Coconut Curry Sauce

30 MINUTES · GLUTEN-FREE · NUT-FREE · SERVES 4

PREP TIME: 10 minutes
TOTAL COOK TIME: 20 minutes
APPROX. PRESSURE BUILD: 8 to 9 minutes
PRESSURE COOK: 3 minutes
PRESSURE RELEASE: 1 minute

2 pounds mussels

8 tablespoons (1 stick) unsalted butter

1 shallot, finely chopped

2 garlic cloves, minced

½ cup dry white wine

1 (14-ounce) can coconut milk

½ cup chicken broth, store-bought or homemade (page 170)

1½ tablespoons curry powder

½ teaspoon salt

Mussels cook to perfection in a savory coconut curry sauce that you'll be tempted to eat with a spoon (I know this from experience!). I like to serve this as an appetizer with French bread for dipping so that we can savor every last bite of both the mussels and the sauce.

1. Rinse the mussels under cold water in a colander. Inspect the mussels and discard any that are open or cracked. If any "beards" (the thin, sticky membrane around the edge) remain, pull them off.

2. Select the sauté function on the pressure cooker (if using an electric pressure cooker; for stovetop pressure cookers, heat over a burner on medium-high heat). Melt the butter in the pot. Add the shallot and garlic and sauté for 2 minutes.

3. Add the white wine and sauté for 3 minutes. Stir with a wooden spoon and scrape any browned bits from the bottom of the pot. Press cancel or turn off the burner.

4. Stir in the coconut milk, chicken broth, curry powder, and salt until well combined. Add the cleaned mussels to the pot and stir to coat them with the sauce.

5. Close and lock the pressure cooker lid, make sure the pressure/steam-release switch is set to sealing, and set the cooking time to 3 minutes at high/normal pressure (if using an electric pressure cooker; for stovetop pressure cookers, heat over a burner on high heat, set a timer for 3 minutes after the pot has reached pressure, then reduce the heat to low). It will take 8 to 9 minutes for the pot to come to pressure before the cooking time begins.

6. After the pressure cooking time ends, electric pressure cookers will automatically turn off their heat (stovetop pressure cookers must be removed from the heat). Release the pressure using the manufacturer's quick-release method.

7. Serve the mussels immediately in their sauce.

PER SERVING: Calories: 558; Total Fat: 50g; Saturated Fat: 36g; Cholesterol: 82mg; Sodium: 785mg; Carbohydrates: 15g; Fiber: 5g; Protein: 13g

15-Minute Mediterranean Halibut

30 MINUTES • DAIRY-FREE • GLUTEN-FREE • NUT-FREE • SERVES 4

PREP TIME: 5 minutes

TOTAL COOK TIME:
15 minutes

APPROX. PRESSURE BUILD:
7 to 8 minutes

PRESSURE COOK: 3 minutes

PRESSURE RELEASE:
1 minute

1 (14.5-ounce) can diced
tomatoes

¼ cup pitted
kalamata olives

1 tablespoon fresh
lemon juice

1½ teaspoons capers

¾ teaspoon dried oregano

4 (4-ounce) halibut fillets

Salt

Freshly ground
black pepper

This meal is not only incredibly quick to make, but it is also low in calories and loaded with nutrients like protein, vitamin D, and omega-3 fatty acids. If you don't love the flavor of halibut, you can easily substitute cod, haddock, or flounder. Make this dish for lunch or dinner—it's only 15 minutes to a delicious meal.

1. Pour the diced tomatoes with their juices into the pressure cooker pot and add the olives, lemon juice, capers, and oregano.
2. Lay the halibut fillets on top of the tomato mixture and season with salt and pepper.
3. Close and lock the pressure cooker lid, make sure the pressure/steam-release switch is set to sealing, and set the cooking time to 3 minutes at high/normal pressure (if using an electric pressure cooker; for stovetop pressure cookers, heat over a burner on high heat, set a timer for 3 minutes after the pot has reached pressure, then reduce the heat to low). It will take 7 to 8 minutes for the pot to come to pressure before the cooking time begins.

4. After the pressure cooking time ends, electric pressure cookers will automatically turn off their heat (stovetop pressure cookers must be removed from the heat). Release the pressure using the manufacturer's quick-release method.

PER SERVING: Calories: 190; Total Fat: 4g; Saturated Fat: 0g; Cholesterol: 53mg; Sodium: 230mg; Carbohydrates: 5g; Fiber: 2g; Protein: 32g

SERVING TIP

This fish is delicious served with orzo or couscous to continue the Mediterranean theme; however, rice is a great side dish for the meal as well.

Ginger-Soy Poached Salmon

30 MINUTES • DAIRY-FREE • NUT-FREE • SERVES 4

PREP TIME: 5 minutes

TOTAL COOK TIME:
15 minutes

APPROX. PRESSURE BUILD:
4 minutes

PRESSURE COOK: 3 minutes

PRESSURE RELEASE:
5 minutes

2 tablespoons toasted
sesame oil

4 (4-ounce) salmon fillets

Salt

Freshly ground
black pepper

Garlic powder

2 teaspoons grated
fresh ginger

¼ cup soy sauce

2 tablespoons rice
wine vinegar

¼ cup chopped scallions
(green parts only)

*This quick salmon dish is great for either lunch or
dinner and is especially delicious when served with
rice and a seaweed salad. While pressure cooking,
the fresh ginger infuses its flavor into the fish, as
the soy sauce and vinegar blend steams it. The result
is a flaky, fork-tender salmon fillet that's bursting
with flavor.*

1. Select the sauté function on the pressure cooker (if
   using an electric pressure cooker; for stovetop pressure
   cookers, heat over a burner on medium-high heat). Heat
   the sesame oil in the pot.
2. Season the salmon with salt, pepper, and garlic powder.
   Press the ginger onto the tops of the salmon fillets.
3. Add the salmon fillets to the pot, skin-side up if they
   have skin, and sear for 2 minutes on each side. Transfer
   the fillets to a plate.
4. Add the soy sauce and vinegar to the pot and
   stir, scraping the bottom of the pot to loosen any
   browned bits.
5. Place a steamer rack trivet in the bottom of the pressure
   cooker pot and place the salmon fillets on the trivet.
   Scatter the scallions over the fillets.

6. Close and lock the pressure cooker lid, make sure the pressure/steam-release switch is set to sealing, and set the cooking time to 3 minutes at high/normal pressure (if using an electric pressure cooker; for stovetop pressure cookers, heat over a burner on high heat, set a timer for 3 minutes after the pot has reached pressure, then reduce the heat to low). It will take about 4 minutes for the pot to come to pressure before the cooking time begins.

7. After the pressure cooking time ends, electric pressure cookers will automatically turn off their heat (stovetop pressure cookers must be removed from the heat). Allow the pressure to release from the pot naturally for 5 minutes before releasing the remaining pressure using the manufacturer's quick-release method.

8. Serve the salmon with the sauce poured over the top.

PER SERVING: Calories: 279; Total Fat: 19g; Saturated Fat: 4g; Cholesterol: 65mg; Sodium: 1004mg; Carbohydrates: 2g; Fiber: 0g; Protein: 23g

COOKING TIP

If you have the time, marinate the salmon in the soy sauce and vinegar mixture with the ginger for 20 minutes before cooking.

Lemon Pepper Salmon with Green Beans

30 MINUTES • GLUTEN-FREE • KETO • NUT-FREE • SERVES 4

PREP TIME: 5 minutes
TOTAL COOK TIME: 15 minutes
APPROX. PRESSURE BUILD: 5 minutes plus 3 minutes
PRESSURE COOK: 2 minutes plus 1 minute
PRESSURE RELEASE: 1 minute

1 cup water

4 (4-ounce) salmon fillets

1 lemon, halved

Coarse salt

Freshly ground black pepper

12 ounces green beans, trimmed

1 tablespoon unsalted butter, cut into small chunks, at room temperature

Lemon pepper seasoning

If you're looking to add more fish to your diet and need something light and quick, this recipe is for you. Salmon is a great source of protein and is packed with nutrients. The green beans in this dish are loaded with vitamins, too, and the tangy lemon pepper seasoning complements both the fish and the vegetable. Serve this on its own for lunch or add some rice to make it a complete dinner.

1. Pour the water into the pressure cooker pot and place a steamer rack trivet in the bottom.
2. Place the salmon fillets in a steamer basket, then put the basket on the trivet in the pressure cooker.
3. Squeeze the juice from the lemon halves over the top of the salmon, then season generously with salt and black pepper.
4. Close and lock the pressure cooker lid, make sure the pressure/steam-release switch is set to sealing, and set the cooking time to 2 minutes at high/normal pressure (if using an electric pressure cooker; for stovetop pressure cookers, heat over a burner on high heat, set a timer for 2 minutes after the pot has reached pressure, then reduce the heat to low). It will take 5 minutes for the pot to come to pressure before the cooking time begins.
5. After the pressure cooking time ends, electric pressure cookers will automatically turn off their heat (stovetop pressure cookers must be removed from the heat). Release the pressure using the manufacturer's quick-release method.

6. Open the lid and add the green beans to the steamer basket, scattering them around the salmon. Add the chunks of butter over the green beans, then season everything with lemon pepper.

7. Close, lock, and seal the lid again, and set the cooking time to 1 minute at high/normal pressure (if using an electric pressure cooker; for stovetop pressure cookers, heat over a burner on high heat, set a timer for 1 minute after the pot has reached pressure, then reduce the heat to low). It will take about 3 minutes for the pot to reach pressure the second time.

8. After the pressure cooking time ends, electric pressure cookers will automatically turn off their heat (stovetop pressure cookers must be removed from the heat). Release the pressure using the manufacturer's quick-release method again.

PER SERVING: Calories: 256; Total Fat: 15g; Saturated Fat: 4g; Cholesterol: 73mg; Sodium: 107mg; Carbohydrates: 7g; Fiber: 3g; Protein: 24g

COOKING TIP

If your salmon fillets are on the thicker side, increase the first pressure cooking time to 3 minutes.

Shrimp Scampi

30 MINUTES • GLUTEN-FREE • KETO • NUT-FREE • SERVES 4

PREP TIME: 5 minutes

TOTAL COOK TIME:
15 minutes

APPROX. PRESSURE BUILD:
4 minutes

PRESSURE COOK: 1 to
2 minutes

PRESSURE RELEASE:
1 minute

4 tablespoons (½ stick)
unsalted butter, divided

1 shallot, finely chopped

2 garlic cloves, minced

½ cup dry white wine

½ cup chicken broth,
store-bought or homemade
(page 170)

½ teaspoon salt

¼ teaspoon freshly ground
black pepper

1 pound large shrimp,
peeled and deveined

2 tablespoons chopped
fresh parsley

My family likes to eat this light and buttery shrimp with linguine and garlic bread as a meal, but it also makes a fantastic appetizer served with slices of baguette. Or skip the pasta and bread for a delicious keto meal—on its own or with vegetables on the side.

1. Select the sauté function on the pressure cooker (if using an electric pressure cooker; for stovetop pressure cookers, heat over a burner on medium-high heat). Melt 2 tablespoons of butter in the pot.

2. Add the shallot and garlic and sauté for 2 minutes.

3. Stir in the white wine, scraping the bottom of the pot to loosen any browned bits. Allow the white wine to cook for 3 minutes, then press cancel or turn off the burner.

4. Stir in the chicken broth, salt, and pepper; then add the shrimp to the pot.

5. Close and lock the pressure cooker lid, make sure the pressure/steam-release switch is set to sealing, and set the cooking time to 1 or 2 minutes at high/normal pressure (if using an electric pressure cooker and depending on how fast your pressure cooker usually cooks; for stovetop pressure cookers, heat over a burner on high heat, set a timer for 1 minute after the pot has reached pressure, then reduce the heat to low). It will take about 4 minutes for the pot to come to pressure before the cooking time begins.

6. After the pressure cooking time ends, electric pressure cookers will automatically turn off their heat (stovetop pressure cookers must be removed from the heat). Release the pressure using the manufacturer's quick-release method.

7. Open the lid and stir in the parsley and remaining 2 tablespoons of butter until the butter is melted.

PER SERVING: Calories: 227; Total Fat: 12g; Saturated Fat: 7g; Cholesterol: 193mg; Sodium: 613mg; Carbohydrates: 4g; Fiber: 0g; Protein: 22g

SERVING TIP

For a low-carb meal, serve with vegetable noodles (either spaghetti squash or spiralized zucchini) instead of pasta.

Low Country Boil

30 MINUTES • DAIRY-FREE • GLUTEN-FREE • NUT-FREE • SERVES 8

PREP TIME: 5 minutes

TOTAL COOK TIME:
30 minutes

APPROX. PRESSURE BUILD:
12 minutes plus 7 minutes

PRESSURE COOK: 5 minutes

PRESSURE RELEASE:
2 minutes

2 cups water

1 pound red potatoes (cut in half if large)

2 ears corn, husks and silk removed, cut into thirds

1 (14-ounce) package smoked sausages, cut into 2-inch chunks

1 bay leaf

4½ teaspoons Old Bay seasoning or Cajun spice blend, divided

2 pounds large shrimp, unpeeled

1 teaspoon Tabasco or your favorite hot sauce

1 pound large shrimp, peeled and deveined

1 pound crab leg and claw pieces (including shells)

Steamed white rice, for serving

It was a dream come true for my husband and me when we realized we could have our own mini Low Country Boil any day of the week thanks to our pressure cooker. Previously a tradition reserved for holidays or cookouts, you can enjoy the spicy Cajun-style shrimp, sausage, potatoes, and corn anytime and with very little effort.

1. Pour the water into the pressure cooker pot and place a steamer rack trivet in the bottom.
2. Put the potatoes, corn, sausage, and bay leaf in a large steamer basket and place the basket on the trivet in the pressure cooker. Sprinkle 4 teaspoons of Old Bay over everything.
3. Close and lock the pressure cooker lid, make sure the pressure/steam-release switch is set to sealing, and set the cooking time to 5 minutes at high/normal pressure (if using an electric pressure cooker; for stovetop pressure cookers, heat over a burner on high heat, set a timer for 5 minutes after the pot has reached pressure, then reduce the heat to low). It will take about 12 minutes for the pot to come to pressure before the cooking time begins.
4. After the pressure cooking time ends, release the pressure using the manufacturer's quick-release method.
5. Open the lid and add the shrimp to the pot on top of the sausage and vegetable mixture. Sprinkle with the remaining ½ teaspoon of Old Bay and the hot sauce.

For a traditional Low Country Boil, we line the table with butcher paper and spread out the shrimp, potatoes, corn, and sausage on it so our guests can dig in with their hands. Set a large bowl nearby for people to discard their shrimp shells and corncobs.

6. Close, lock, and seal the lid again, and set the cooking time to 0 minutes at high/normal pressure (if using an electric pressure cooker; for stovetop pressure cookers, heat over a burner on high heat once more, then remove the pressure cooker from the heat as soon as the pot reaches pressure). It will take about 7 minutes for the pot to reach pressure the second time.

7. After the pressure cooking time ends, electric pressure cookers will automatically turn off their heat (stovetop pressure cookers must be removed from the heat). Release the pressure using the manufacturer's quick-release method again.

8. Open the lid and pour the contents of the steamer basket into a large bowl. Remove the bay leaf. Pour the liquid from the bottom of the pressure cooker into the bowl and toss to coat everything evenly.

9. Pour the contents of the bowl into a large colander in the sink and strain out the liquid, then return the shrimp, sausage, and vegetables to the bowl and serve.

PER SERVING: Calories: 315; Total fat: 14g; Saturated Fat: 5g; Cholesterol: 193mg; Sodium: 760mg; Carbohydrates: 20g; Fiber: 2g; Protein: 30g

New Orleans Barbecue Shrimp

30 MINUTES • NUT-FREE • SERVES 4

PREP TIME: 5 minutes

TOTAL COOK TIME:
10 minutes

APPROX. PRESSURE BUILD:
6 minutes

PRESSURE COOK: 0 minutes

PRESSURE RELEASE:
1 minute

½ cup Worcestershire sauce

2 tablespoons fresh
lemon juice

2 teaspoons freshly ground
black pepper

2 teaspoons Cajun
seasoning

½ teaspoon Tabasco or
your favorite hot sauce

2 garlic cloves, minced

1½ cups (3 sticks) unsalted
butter, at room temperature

1 pound large shrimp,
unpeeled

One of my favorite food cities in the world is New Orleans, and my favorite meal there is barbecue shrimp. Don't let the name fool you: The shrimp isn't grilled with a sweet barbecue sauce; it's simmered in the most heavenly combo of butter and Worcestershire sauce—it's so good you'll definitely want some French bread on the side to sop up the extra sauce. In New Orleans you eat these with your hands (even at upscale restaurants), so be ready to roll up your sleeves and wear a bib if you have one!

1. Mix the Worcestershire sauce, lemon juice, pepper, Cajun seasoning, hot sauce, and garlic together in the pressure cooker pot. Place the sticks of butter in the sauce.

2. Close and lock the pressure cooker lid, make sure the pressure/steam-release switch is set to sealing, and set the cooking time to 0 minutes at high/normal pressure (if using an electric pressure cooker; for stovetop pressure cookers, heat over a burner on high heat, then remove the pressure cooker from the heat as soon as the pot reaches pressure). It will take about 6 minutes for the pot to come to pressure before the cooking time begins.

3. After the pressure cooking time ends, release the pressure using the manufacturer's quick-release method.

4. Select the sauté function on the pressure cooker (if using an electric pressure cooker; for stovetop pressure cookers, heat over a burner on medium-high heat). Add the shrimp and sauté until pink and opaque, about 2 minutes—watch closely after the first minute so the shrimp doesn't overcook. Press cancel or turn off the burner and quickly remove the pot from the heat.

5. Serve the shrimp with the butter sauce in bowls.

PER SERVING: Calories: 738; Total Fat: 69g; Saturated Fat: 44g; Cholesterol: 345mg; Sodium: 993mg; Carbohydrates: 9g; Fiber: 0g; Protein: 22g

Seafood Gumbo

NUT-FREE • SERVES 6

PREP TIME: 10 minutes

TOTAL COOK TIME:
20 minutes

APPROX. PRESSURE BUILD:
12 minutes

PRESSURE COOK: 4 minutes

PRESSURE RELEASE:
1 minute

8 tablespoons (1 stick)
unsalted butter

½ cup all-purpose flour

1 medium onion, chopped

1 green bell pepper, seeded
and chopped

2 celery stalks, chopped

3 garlic cloves, minced

4 cups seafood or
fish broth

1 (14.5-ounce) can diced
tomatoes

2 cups frozen sliced okra

1 teaspoon Cajun seasoning

1 teaspoon salt

½ teaspoon freshly ground
black pepper

¼ teaspoon ground
white pepper

⅛ teaspoon
cayenne pepper

1 pound large shrimp,
peeled and deveined

1 pound crab leg and claw
pieces (including shells)

Cajun and Creole cuisine have always been among my favorites and have inspired my cooking since I was a teen. Gumbo is a staple of both Cajun and Creole cooking and, like many stews, it comes out perfectly in the pressure cooker. This recipe is inspired by my favorite gumbo from the Gumbo Shop restaurant in New Orleans. Like many Cajun dishes, this one starts with a roux (a golden flour-and-butter base), which can be prepared directly in your pressure cooker pot.

1. Select the sauté function on the pressure cooker (if using an electric pressure cooker; for stovetop pressure cookers, heat over a burner on medium-high heat). Melt the butter in the pot. Slowly whisk in the flour. Continue cooking and whisking until the roux is the color of peanut butter, about 5 minutes.

2. Add the onion, bell pepper, celery, and garlic to the roux and sauté until the vegetables are tender, about 5 minutes.

3. Add the broth to the pot and stir with a wooden spoon, scraping the bottom of the pot to loosen any browned bits. Press cancel or turn off the burner.

4. Add the diced tomatoes with their juices, frozen okra, Cajun seasoning, salt, black pepper, white pepper, and cayenne pepper and stir well.

5. Close and lock the pressure cooker lid, make sure the pressure/steam-release switch is set to sealing, and set the cooking time to 4 minutes at high/normal pressure (if using an electric pressure cooker; for stovetop pressure cookers, heat over a burner on high heat, set a timer for 4 minutes after the pot has reached pressure, then reduce the heat to low). It will take about

12 minutes for the pot to come to pressure before the cooking time begins.

6. After the pressure cooking time ends, electric pressure cookers will automatically turn off their heat (stovetop pressure cookers must be removed from the heat). Release the pressure using the manufacturer's quick-release method.

7. Open the lid and stir in the shrimp and crab pieces. Quickly close and seal the lid and allow the seafood to cook in the pot's residual heat (do not bring the pot to pressure or sauté again) for 10 minutes.

8. Serve over steamed white rice.

PER SERVING: Calories: 368; Total Fat: 18g; Saturated Fat: 10g; Cholesterol: 264mg; Sodium: 897mg; Carbohydrates: 17g; Fiber: 3g; Protein: 34g

COOKING TIP

I recommend prepping all the ingredients (chopping and measuring) before the cooking starts. There are some points while cooking this recipe where things move rather quickly, and you'll be glad to have everything ready to go.

7

POULTRY

Asian-Style Orange-Soy Chicken

30 MINUTES • DAIRY-FREE • NUT-FREE • SERVES 4

PREP TIME: 5 minutes

TOTAL COOK TIME:
25 minutes

APPROX. PRESSURE BUILD:
5 minutes

PRESSURE COOK: 7 minutes

PRESSURE RELEASE:
5 minutes

1 pound boneless, skinless chicken breasts, cut into strips

2 garlic cloves, minced

2 scallions, chopped (green parts only)

1 tablespoon toasted sesame oil

¼ cup plus 2 tablespoons orange juice, divided

¼ cup soy sauce

1 teaspoon grated orange zest

2 tablespoons cornstarch

I love the flavor of orange chicken from Chinese take-out restaurants as a treat, but I try not to indulge in it too often. This lighter version is not breaded or fried but rather sautéed with a coating of delicious orange sauce. The recipe is on a regular rotation in our house as a quick weeknight dinner option. Serve over white or brown rice, perhaps with steamed broccoli on the side.

1. In a medium bowl, toss the chicken with the garlic and scallions. Set aside while you prep the rest of the ingredients.

2. Select the sauté function on the pressure cooker (if using an electric pressure cooker; for stovetop pressure cookers, heat over a burner on medium-high heat). Heat the sesame oil in the pot.

3. Add the chicken with the garlic and scallions to the pot. Sauté until the chicken is browned on all sides, 3 to 4 minutes.

4. Pour ¼ cup of orange juice into the pot and scrape the bottom of the pot with a wooden spoon to loosen any browned bits. Stir in the soy sauce and orange zest. Press cancel or turn off the burner.

5. Close and lock the pressure cooker lid, make sure the pressure/steam-release switch is set to sealing, and set the cooking time to 7 minutes at high/normal pressure (if using an electric pressure cooker; for stovetop pressure cookers, heat over a burner on high heat, set a timer for 7 minutes after the pot has reached pressure, then reduce the heat to low). It will take about 5 minutes for the pot to come to pressure before the cooking time begins.

6. After the pressure cooking time ends, electric pressure cookers will automatically turn off their heat (stovetop pressure cookers must be removed from the heat). Allow the pressure to release from the pot naturally for 5 minutes before releasing the remaining pressure using the manufacturer's quick-release method.

7. While the pressure is releasing, in a small bowl, whisk together the cornstarch and remaining 2 tablespoons of orange juice to make a slurry.

8. Open the lid, select the sauté function on the pot again, and whisk in the slurry. Simmer until the sauce thickens, 1 to 2 minutes, then press cancel or turn off the burner.

PER SERVING: Calories: 158; Total Fat: 2g; Saturated Fat: 0g; Cholesterol: 65mg; Sodium: 976mg; Carbohydrates: 8g; Fiber: 1g; Protein: 27g

Chicken Florentine

NUT-FREE · SERVES 4

PREP TIME: 10 minutes
TOTAL COOK TIME: 50 minutes
APPROX. PRESSURE BUILD: 8 minutes
PRESSURE COOK: 8 minutes
PRESSURE RELEASE: 25 minutes

2 tablespoons olive oil

1 pound boneless, skinless chicken breasts, cut into bite-size pieces

½ teaspoon garlic powder, plus more for seasoning

½ teaspoon salt, plus more for seasoning

¼ teaspoon freshly ground black pepper, plus more for seasoning

⅓ cup finely chopped onion

1½ cups chicken broth, store-bought or homemade (page 170)

1 cup heavy cream

3 cups baby spinach

8 ounces uncooked linguine, broken in half

¾ cup grated Parmesan cheese

When you see "Florentine" in the name of a dish, it usually means that the dish contains spinach. While chicken or fish Florentine is usually topped with a creamy spinach sauce, this pressure-cooked pasta has the chicken, sauce, spinach, and pasta cook together in one pot. Our family has found that this dish makes delicious leftovers, as the sauce thickens further and the ingredients blend together even more after a night in the fridge.

1. Select the sauté function on the pressure cooker (if using an electric pressure cooker; for stovetop pressure cookers, heat over a burner on medium-high heat). Heat the olive oil in the pot.

2. Season the chicken with garlic powder, salt, and pepper. Add the chicken to the pot, along with the onion, and sauté for 4 minutes.

3. Stir in the chicken broth, scraping the bottom of the pot with a wooden spoon to loosen any browned bits. Add the heavy cream, spinach, and remaining ½ teaspoon garlic powder, ½ teaspoon salt, and ¼ teaspoon pepper and stir to combine. Press cancel or turn off the burner.

4. Add the linguine to the pot and mix to coat it in the sauce.

5. Close and lock the pressure cooker lid, make sure the pressure/steam-release switch is set to sealing, and set the cooking time to 8 minutes at high/normal pressure (if using an electric pressure cooker; for stovetop pressure cookers, heat over a burner on high heat, set a

timer for 8 minutes after the pot has reached pressure, then reduce the heat to low). It will take 7 to 8 minutes for the pot to come to pressure before the cooking time begins.

6. After the pressure cooking time ends, electric pressure cookers will automatically turn off their heat (stovetop pressure cookers must be removed from the heat). Allow the pressure to release from the pot naturally, 20 to 25 minutes.

7. Open the lid and select the sauté function on the pot again. Stir well to break up any linguine that may be stuck together. Gradually stir in the Parmesan cheese and simmer, stirring occasionally, until the cheese is melted and the sauce thickens, about 5 minutes. Press cancel or turn off the burner. The sauce will continue to thicken as it cools.

PER SERVING: Calories: 636; Total Fat: 37g; Saturated Fat: 18g; Cholesterol: 203mg; Sodium: 885mg; Carbohydrates: 35g; Fiber: 0g; Protein: 42g

COOKING TIP

To make this dish low carb, you can skip the pasta and serve with vegetables on the side. If you're not using pasta, reduce the chicken broth to 1 cup and cook for 4 minutes on high pressure with a 10-minute natural pressure release.

Chicken Piccata

30 MINUTES • NUT-FREE • SERVES 4

PREP TIME: 5 minutes
TOTAL COOK TIME: 30 minutes
APPROX. PRESSURE BUILD: 6 to 7 minutes
PRESSURE COOK: 10 minutes
PRESSURE RELEASE: 1 minute

2 boneless, skinless chicken breasts

Salt

Freshly ground black pepper

¼ cup all-purpose flour

2 tablespoons vegetable oil

¼ cup dry white wine

1 teaspoon minced garlic

½ cup chicken broth, store-bought or homemade (page 170)

2 tablespoons fresh lemon juice

1 tablespoon capers

2 tablespoons unsalted butter, at room temperature

Light and lemony chicken piccata is one of our family's go-to meals. It doesn't require many ingredients and the whole family loves its fresh, zesty flavor. We serve it with steamed white rice, but it's also wonderful with linguine and vegetables like broccoli or asparagus.

1. Cut the chicken breasts in half horizontally so that you have 4 thin chicken cutlets. Season both sides with salt and pepper.
2. Put the flour in a shallow dish and dredge the chicken cutlets, one by one, in the flour, shaking off any excess.
3. Select the sauté function on the pressure cooker (if using an electric pressure cooker; for stovetop pressure cookers, heat over a burner on medium-high heat). Heat the vegetable oil in the pot.
4. Add the chicken cutlets to the pot (you may need to do this in two batches) and sear for 2 minutes on each side. Transfer the chicken to a plate.
5. Stir in the white wine, scraping the bottom of the pot to loosen any browned bits. Allow the white wine to cook for 1 minute, then add the garlic and cook for 1 minute more, stirring constantly.
6. Stir in the chicken broth, lemon juice, and capers and bring to a boil. Press cancel or turn off the burner.
7. Place the chicken cutlets on top of the broth mixture in the pot.

You can get more mileage out of this recipe by substituting salmon for the chicken. Follow the same instructions (including the flour dredging and searing) except cook the salmon on a trivet over the sauce for 3 minutes at high pressure with a 5-minute natural pressure release. Voilà!

8. Close and lock the pressure cooker lid, make sure the pressure/steam-release switch is set to sealing, and set the cooking time to 10 minutes at high/normal pressure (if using an electric pressure cooker; for stovetop pressure cookers, heat over a burner on high heat, set a timer for 8 minutes after the pot has reached pressure, then reduce the heat to low). It will take 6 to 7 minutes for the pot to come to pressure before the cooking time begins.

9. After the pressure cooking time ends, electric pressure cookers will automatically turn off their heat (stovetop pressure cookers must be removed from the heat). Release the pressure using the manufacturer's quick-release method.

10. Open the lid and select the sauté function on the pot again. Stir in the butter until it is melted. Press cancel or turn off the burner.

PER SERVING: Calories: 234; Total Fat: 16g; Saturated Fat: 5g; Cholesterol: 59mg; Sodium: 244mg; Carbohydrates: 7g; Fiber: 0g; Protein: 18g

Mississippi Chicken Thighs

30 MINUTES • NUT-FREE • SERVES 4 TO 5

PREP TIME: 5 minutes

TOTAL COOK TIME:
30 minutes

APPROX. PRESSURE BUILD:
4 to 5 minutes

PRESSURE COOK: 10 minutes

PRESSURE RELEASE:
5 minutes

1 tablespoon vegetable oil

4 or 5 bone-in, skin-on
chicken thighs

1 cup chicken broth,
store-bought or homemade
(page 170)

1 (1-ounce) packet au jus
gravy mix

1 (1-ounce) packet ranch
seasoning mix

2 tablespoons unsalted
butter, cut into small
chunks, at room
temperature

8 pickled
pepperoncini peppers

*We are fans of the pepperoncini-topped
Mississippi-style pot roast and like to use the same
signature ingredients with other meats, too. This
variation uses chicken thighs and is made quickly in
the pressure cooker.*

1. Select the sauté function on the pressure cooker (if
   using an electric pressure cooker; for stovetop pressure
   cookers, heat over a burner on medium-high heat).
   Heat the vegetable oil in the pot.
2. Add the chicken thighs to the pot and sauté until
   browned, 3 to 4 minutes per side. Transfer the chicken
   to a plate.
3. Stir in the chicken broth, scraping the bottom of the
   pot to loosen any browned bits. Press cancel or turn off
   the burner.
4. Return the chicken thighs to the pot, putting them
   directly in the broth. Pour the packets of au jus gravy
   mix and ranch seasoning mix over the top of the
   chicken. Scatter the chunks of butter and pepperoncini
   peppers on top of the chicken.

5. Close and lock the pressure cooker lid, make sure the pressure/steam-release switch is set to sealing, and set the cooking time to 10 minutes at high/normal pressure (if using an electric pressure cooker; for stovetop pressure cookers, heat over a burner on high heat, set a timer for 10 minutes after the pot has reached pressure, then reduce the heat to low). It will take 4 to 5 minutes for the pot to come to pressure before the cooking time begins.

6. After the pressure cooking time ends, electric pressure cookers will automatically turn off their heat (stovetop pressure cookers must be removed from the heat). Allow the pressure to release from the pot naturally for 5 minutes before releasing the remaining pressure using the manufacturer's quick-release method.

7. Serve the chicken with some of the broth from the pot poured over the top.

PER SERVING: Calories: 378; Total Fat: 30g; Saturated Fat: 11g; Cholesterol: 120mg; Sodium: 2765mg; Carbohydrates: 8g; Fiber: 0g; Protein: 20g

INGREDIENT TIP

I use bone-in, skin-on chicken thighs for added flavor, but you can substitute boneless, skinless chicken thighs. If you are using boneless, skinless thighs, double the butter to 4 tablespoons.

Japanese Chicken Curry

DAIRY-FREE · NUT-FREE · SERVES 6

PREP TIME: 10 minutes

TOTAL COOK TIME:
35 minutes

APPROX. PRESSURE BUILD:
12 minutes

PRESSURE COOK: 15 minutes

PRESSURE RELEASE:
1 minute

1 tablespoon vegetable oil

2 pounds boneless, skinless chicken breasts, cut into 1-inch pieces

1 medium onion, sliced

2 large potatoes, peeled and cut into 1½-inch pieces

2 carrots, peeled and chopped

2½ cups chicken broth, store-bought or homemade (page 170)

2 tablespoons soy sauce

1 (4-ounce) package Japanese curry mix

A big part of my family is Japanese, so I've always been partial to the flavor of Japanese curry, having grown up with it. Japanese curry has a milder flavor than Indian and Thai curries (which are also delicious). This dish is a family favorite, and leftovers store and freeze well.

1. Select the sauté function on the pressure cooker (if using an electric pressure cooker; for stovetop pressure cookers, heat over a burner on medium-high heat). Heat the oil in the pot.

2. Add the chicken and onion to the pot and stir well to coat in oil. Sauté, stirring occasionally, until the chicken is mostly white on the outside, about 5 minutes.

3. Add the potatoes and carrots and stir well. Sauté with the chicken and onion for 1 minute.

4. Stir the chicken broth and soy sauce into the chicken mixture. Break up the brick of curry mix and lay the pieces over the top of the chicken mixture—do not mix them in. Press cancel or turn off the burner.

5. Close and lock the pressure cooker lid, make sure the pressure/steam-release switch is set to sealing, and set the cooking time to 15 minutes at high/normal pressure (if using an electric pressure cooker; for stovetop pressure cookers, heat over a burner on high heat, set a timer for 15 minutes after the pot has reached pressure, then reduce the heat to low). It will take about 12 minutes for the pot to come to pressure before the cooking time begins.

6. After the pressure cooking time ends, electric pressure cookers will automatically turn off their heat (stovetop pressure cookers must be removed from the heat). Release the pressure using the manufacturer's quick-release method.

7. Stir the curry well. The sauce will thicken as it stands.

PER SERVING: Calories: 351; Total Fat: 11g; Saturated Fat: 1g; Cholesterol: 93mg; Sodium: 164mg; Carbohydrates: 34g; Fiber: 10g; Protein: 41g

INGREDIENT TIP

You can find Japanese curry mix in the international or Asian section of your grocery store. The two most common brands are Vermont Curry and S&B Golden Curry, and you can choose from mild, medium, or hot curry mixes depending on your taste.

Easy One-Pot Chicken and Rice

30 MINUTES · DAIRY-FREE · GLUTEN-FREE · NUT-FREE · SERVES 4

PREP TIME: 5 minutes	
TOTAL COOK TIME: 30 minutes	
APPROX. PRESSURE BUILD: 7 minutes	
PRESSURE COOK: 7 minutes	
PRESSURE RELEASE: 10 minutes	

1½ tablespoons olive oil

1 pound boneless, skinless chicken breasts, cut into bite-size pieces

1½ cups chicken broth, store-bought or homemade (page 170)

1 cup long-grain white rice, rinsed until the water runs clear

½ teaspoon salt

¼ teaspoon freshly ground black pepper

¼ teaspoon garlic powder

1 cup frozen mixed vegetables

A perfect solution for busy weeknights, this one-pot meal uses a shortcut of frozen mixed vegetables to minimize prep time—choose whatever combination you like. The meal stores well, too, so you can make it in advance and keep it in the refrigerator for a few days and then serve it on a night when you know you'll be short on time. It goes great with a tossed salad on the side.

1. Select the sauté function on the pressure cooker (if using an electric pressure cooker; for stovetop pressure cookers, heat over a burner on medium-high heat). Heat the olive oil in the pot.

2. Add the chicken to the pot and sauté until the edges are lightly browned, 3 to 4 minutes. Press cancel or turn off the burner and transfer the chicken to a plate.

3. Stir the chicken broth into the pot and use a wooden spoon to scrape the bottom of the pot to loosen any browned bits.

4. Stir in the rice, salt, pepper, and garlic powder. Add the frozen vegetables and chicken chunks on top of the rice mixture.

5. Close and lock the pressure cooker lid, make sure the pressure/steam-release switch is set to sealing, and set the cooking time to 7 minutes at high/normal pressure (if using an electric pressure cooker; for stovetop pressure cookers, heat over a burner on high heat, set a timer for 7 minutes after the pot has reached pressure, then reduce the heat to low). It will take about 7 minutes for the pot to come to pressure before the cooking time begins.

6. After the pressure cooking time ends, electric pressure cookers will automatically turn off their heat (stovetop pressure cookers must be removed from the heat). Allow the pressure to release from the pot naturally for 10 minutes before releasing the remaining pressure using the manufacturer's quick-release method.

7. Open the lid, stir the contents, and fluff the rice.

PER SERVING: Calories: 342; Total Fat: 9g; Saturated Fat: 1g; Cholesterol: 74mg; Sodium: 433mg; Carbohydrates: 43g; Fiber: 3g; Protein: 33g

Quick Chicken and Dumplings

30 MINUTES • NUT-FREE • SERVES 4 TO 6

PREP TIME: 10 minutes	
TOTAL COOK TIME: 30 minutes	
APPROX. PRESSURE BUILD: 9 minutes	
PRESSURE COOK: 3 minutes	
PRESSURE RELEASE: 10 minutes	

Chicken and dumplings is the perfect comfort-food meal to make on a cold fall or winter day. Instead of waiting hours for it to be prepared in a slow cooker, you can make it in your pressure cooker in a fraction of the time instead! Using refrigerated biscuit dough for the dumplings instead of making them from scratch will get this on your table in about 30 minutes.

1 tablespoon vegetable oil

1 to 1½ pounds boneless, skinless chicken breasts, cut into bite-size pieces

1 medium onion, chopped

3 celery stalks, chopped

3 carrots, peeled and chopped

2½ cups chicken broth, store-bought or homemade (page 170)

½ teaspoon salt

¼ teaspoon freshly ground black pepper

¼ teaspoon garlic powder

1 (10-ounce) can refrigerated biscuit dough, cut into 1-inch pieces

1 tablespoon cornstarch

½ cup heavy cream

1 cup frozen peas

2 tablespoons chopped fresh parsley

1. Select the sauté function on the pressure cooker (if using an electric pressure cooker; for stovetop pressure cookers, heat over a burner on medium-high heat). Heat the vegetable oil in the pot.

2. Add the chicken, onion, celery, and carrots and sauté until the chicken is browned and the vegetables are soft, about 6 minutes. Press cancel or turn off the burner.

3. Stir in the chicken broth and use a wooden spoon to scrape the bottom of the pot to loosen any browned bits.

4. Stir in the salt, pepper, and garlic powder. Place the pieces of biscuit dough on top of the chicken and broth mixture one at a time so that they don't stick together.

5. Close and lock the pressure cooker lid, make sure the pressure/steam-release switch is set to sealing, and set the cooking time to 3 minutes at high/normal pressure (if using an electric pressure cooker; for stovetop pressure cookers, heat over a burner on high heat, set a timer for 3 minutes after the pot has reached pressure, then reduce the heat to low). It will take about 9 minutes for the pot to come to pressure before the cooking time begins.

6. After the pressure cooking time ends, electric pressure cookers will automatically turn off their heat (stovetop pressure cookers must be removed from the heat). Allow the pressure to release from the pot naturally for 10 minutes before releasing the remaining pressure using the manufacturer's quick-release method.

7. While the pressure is releasing, whisk together the cornstarch and heavy cream to make a slurry.

8. After the pressure is released, open the lid, select the sauté function on the pot again, and stir in the slurry until well mixed. Add the frozen peas to the pot and simmer until the sauce thickens and the peas are heated through, about 3 minutes, then press cancel or turn off the burner.

9. Stir in the chopped parsley and serve.

PER SERVING: Calories: 564; Total Fat: 33g; Saturated Fat: 11g; Cholesterol: 118mg; Sodium: 1038mg; Carbohydrates: 45g; Fiber: 5g; Protein: 37g

COOKING TIP

Use a pizza cutter to evenly cut the biscuit dough.

Lemon Pepper Whole Chicken

DAIRY-FREE • GLUTEN-FREE • KETO • NUT-FREE • **SERVES 4**

PREP TIME: 5 minutes

TOTAL COOK TIME: 1 hour 10 minutes

APPROX. PRESSURE BUILD: 4 minutes

PRESSURE COOK: 25 minutes

PRESSURE RELEASE: 25 to 35 minutes

1 (3½- to 4-pound) whole chicken

Coarse salt

Freshly ground black pepper

Garlic powder

3 lemons, divided

1 tablespoon vegetable oil

1 cup chicken broth, store-bought or homemade (page 170)

Once you make a whole chicken in the pressure cooker, you'll never want to roast one in the oven again. The pressure cooker is a hands-off way to make your chicken come out fork-tender and perfectly moist every time. This chicken is great served for dinner or for meal-prepping when you need lots of fresh, rotisserie-style chicken for lunches and snacks.

1. Season the outside of the chicken and inside the cavity with salt, pepper, and garlic powder.

2. Thinly slice one of the lemons. Carefully lift the skin on the breast and back of the chicken and slide the lemon slices underneath.

3. Select the sauté function on the pressure cooker (if using an electric pressure cooker; for stovetop pressure cookers, heat over a burner on medium-high heat). Heat the oil in the pot.

4. Add the chicken, breast-side down, and brown for 3 to 4 minutes, then flip it onto its back and brown for another 3 to 4 minutes. Transfer the chicken to a plate.

5. Add the chicken broth to the pot and scrape the bottom with a wooden spoon to loosen any browned bits. Press cancel or turn off the burner, then squeeze the juice of the second lemon into the pot.

6. Place a steamer rack trivet in the bottom of the pressure cooker pot, then place the chicken, breast-side up, on the trivet. Cut the remaining lemon into wedges and stuff them inside the chicken's cavity.

COOKING TIPS

* This recipe was written for a 6-quart pressure cooker. Add an additional ½ cup of liquid to the bottom of the pot if preparing this in an 8-quart pressure cooker.

* The first step of browning the chicken is optional and more for the texture of a crisper skin than anything. You can skip this step to save time if you are planning to shred the chicken for meal prep.

* If you're not a fan of lemon or just want to change this recipe up, you can season it with your favorite meat or poultry seasonings and skip the lemons and lemon juice. It's a very versatile recipe.

* For chickens larger than 4 pounds, add an additional 3 minutes of pressure cooking time for each additional half-pound of weight.

7. Close and lock the pressure cooker lid, make sure the pressure/steam-release switch is set to sealing, and set the cooking time to 25 minutes at high/normal pressure (if using an electric pressure cooker; for stovetop pressure cookers, heat over a burner on high heat, set a timer for 25 minutes after the pot has reached pressure, then reduce the heat to low). It will take about 4 minutes for the pot to come to pressure before the cooking time begins.

8. After the pressure cooking time ends, electric pressure cookers will automatically turn off their heat (stovetop pressure cookers must be removed from the heat). Allow the pressure to release from the pot naturally, 25 to 35 minutes.

9. Open the lid and carefully remove the chicken from the pressure cooker. Allow the chicken to rest for 10 minutes before carving.

PER SERVING: Calories: 415; Total Fat: 25g; Saturated Fat: 5g; Cholesterol: 89mg; Sodium: 335mg; Carbohydrates: 3g; Fiber: 0g; Protein: 43g

8

BEEF, PORK, and LAMB

Beef with Broccoli

30 MINUTES • DAIRY-FREE • NUT-FREE • SERVES 4

PREP TIME: 10 minutes

TOTAL COOK TIME:
30 minutes

APPROX. PRESSURE BUILD:
4 minutes plus 7 minutes

PRESSURE COOK: 12 minutes

PRESSURE RELEASE:
2 minutes

½ cup plus 2 tablespoons
water, divided

1 head broccoli, chopped
into florets

2 tablespoons toasted
sesame oil

1½ pounds chuck or flank
steak, cut into thin strips

2 garlic cloves, minced

1 teaspoon grated
fresh ginger

⅓ cup oyster sauce

¼ cup soy sauce

2 tablespoons brown sugar

½ cup beef broth

2 tablespoons cornstarch

*This easy entrée tastes amazing and is much quicker
than ordering takeout. Serve it with white, brown,
or fried rice, or skip the extra starch and add more
veggies like yellow squash, zucchini, and celery along
with the broccoli with the same cooking time.*

1. Pour ½ cup of water into the pressure cooker pot and
place a steamer rack trivet in the bottom.

2. Put the broccoli florets in a steamer basket. Place the
steamer basket on the trivet in the pressure cooker.

3. Close and lock the pressure cooker lid, make sure the
pressure/steam-release switch is set to sealing, and set
the cooking time to 0 minutes at high/normal pressure (if using an electric pressure cooker; for stovetop
pressure cookers, heat over a burner on high heat, then
remove the pressure cooker from the heat as soon as the
pot reaches pressure). It will take 4 minutes for the pot
to come to pressure with an electric pressure cooker and
7 to 8 minutes to come to pressure with a stovetop pressure cooker before the cooking time begins.

4. After the pressure cooking time ends, electric pressure cookers will automatically turn off their heat
(stovetop pressure cookers must be removed from the
heat). Release the pressure using the manufacturer's
quick-release method.

5. Remove the steamer rack basket and trivet from the pot
and set aside. Rinse and dry the pot, then return to the
electric pressure cooker or stovetop.

6. Select the sauté function on the pressure cooker (if
using an electric pressure cooker; for stovetop pressure
cookers, heat over a burner on medium-high heat).
Heat the sesame oil in the pot.

7. Add the steak strips to the pot and sauté until browned, 3 to 4 minutes. Add the garlic and ginger and stir to combine. Sauté for 1 minute. Press cancel or turn off the burner.

8. In a medium bowl, whisk together the oyster sauce, soy sauce, and brown sugar.

9. Pour the beef broth into the pressure cooker pot with the beef and use a wooden spoon to scrape any browned bits from the bottom. Pour the soy sauce mixture over everything and stir to combine.

10. Close, lock, and seal the lid again, and set the cooking time to 12 minutes at high/normal pressure (if using an electric pressure cooker; for stovetop pressure cookers, heat over a burner on high heat once more, set a timer for 12 minutes after the pot has reached pressure, then reduce the heat to low). It will take about 7 minutes for the pot to reach pressure the second time.

11. After the pressure cooking time ends, electric pressure cookers will automatically turn off their heat (stovetop pressure cookers must be removed from the heat). Release the pressure using the manufacturer's quick-release method again.

12. In a small bowl, whisk together the cornstarch and remaining 2 tablespoons of water to make a slurry.

13. Open the lid, select the sauté function on the pot again, and whisk in the slurry. Simmer until the sauce thickens, about 1 minute, then press cancel or turn off the burner. Toss the broccoli with the meat and sauce.

PER SERVING: Calories: 434; Total Fat: 22g; Saturated Fat: 1g; Cholesterol: 85mg; Sodium: 925mg; Carbohydrates: 17g; Fiber: 3g; Protein: 41g

Salisbury Steak with Mushroom Gravy

NUT-FREE • SERVES 4

PREP TIME: 10 minutes	
TOTAL COOK TIME: 55 minutes	
APPROX. PRESSURE BUILD: 8 minutes	
PRESSURE COOK: 15 minutes	
PRESSURE RELEASE: 10 minutes	

Serve this tender ground beef steak and gravy with mashed potatoes and a side of carrots for the quintessential comfort food! The mushroom gravy and meat cook together in the same pan, infusing each other with flavor. I buy presliced cremini mushrooms (also known as baby bellas) to save time on recipe prep.

1 pound ground beef

½ cup crushed butter crackers (such as Ritz)

1 large egg, lightly beaten

1 teaspoon Worcestershire sauce

1 teaspoon salt, divided

½ teaspoon freshly ground black pepper, divided

½ teaspoon garlic powder, divided

¼ teaspoon onion powder

1 tablespoon vegetable oil

2 tablespoons unsalted butter

8 ounces cremini mushrooms, sliced

1 small onion, sliced

2 cups beef broth

1 cup milk

2 tablespoons cornstarch

2 tablespoons water

1. In a medium bowl, combine the ground beef, crushed crackers, egg, Worcestershire sauce, ½ teaspoon of salt, ¼ teaspoon of pepper, ¼ teaspoon of garlic powder, and onion powder until well mixed. Form the meat into 4 even patties, about ½ inch thick, and place on a plate.

2. Select the sauté function on the pressure cooker (if using an electric pressure cooker; for stovetop pressure cookers, heat over a burner on medium-high heat). Heat the vegetable oil in the pot.

3. Add the beef patties to the pot (you may need to do this in two batches) and cook until browned, about 3 minutes per side. Transfer the patties to the same plate.

4. Add the butter to the pot and heat until melted, scraping the bottom of the pot with a wooden spoon to loosen any browned bits.

5. Add the mushrooms and onion to the pot and sauté, stirring occasionally, until soft, 3 to 4 minutes. Press cancel or turn off the burner.

6. Pour the broth and milk into the pot, then stir in the remaining ½ teaspoon of salt, remaining ¼ teaspoon of pepper, and remaining ¼ teaspoon of garlic powder.

7. Return the beef patties to the pot—it is okay if they overlap a bit.

8. Close and lock the pressure cooker lid, make sure the pressure/steam-release switch is set to sealing, and set the cooking time to 15 minutes at high/normal pressure (if using an electric pressure cooker; for stovetop pressure cookers, heat over a burner on high heat, set a timer for 15 minutes after the pot has reached pressure, then reduce the heat to low). It will take about 8 minutes for the pot to come to pressure before the cooking time begins.

9. After the pressure cooking time ends, electric pressure cookers will automatically turn off their heat (stovetop pressure cookers must be removed from the heat). Allow the pressure to release from the pot naturally for 10 minutes before releasing the remaining pressure using the manufacturer's quick-release method.

10. In a small bowl, whisk together the cornstarch and water to make a slurry.

11. Open the lid, remove the steaks from the pot, and place them onto a serving platter. Select the sauté function on the pot again, and stir in the slurry. Simmer until the gravy thickens, about 5 minutes, then press cancel or turn off the burner.

12. Pour the mushroom gravy over the Salisbury steaks and serve.

PER SERVING: Calories: 384; Total Fat: 22g; Saturated Fat: 8g; Cholesterol: 131mg; Sodium: 931mg; Carbohydrates: 18g; Fiber: 2g; Protein: 30g

Corned Beef and Cabbage

DAIRY-FREE • GLUTEN-FREE • NUT-FREE • SERVES 8

PREP TIME: 5 minutes

TOTAL COOK TIME: 2 hours 5 minutes

APPROX. PRESSURE BUILD: 14 minutes plus 15 minutes

PRESSURE COOK: 90 minutes plus 4 minutes

PRESSURE RELEASE: 2 minutes

1 (4-pound) corned beef brisket, with seasoning packet

4 cups water

1 green cabbage, cut into wedges

1½ pounds red potatoes, halved if large

4 carrots, peeled and cut into 3-inch pieces

My family makes corned beef and cabbage every year on St. Patrick's Day. But since we love corned beef so much, we like to stock up on corned beef briskets for our freezer so we can make them whenever we have the craving! Making corned beef in the pressure cooker takes about half the total cooking time compared with boiling it on the stove, and it's much easier since you don't have to monitor it or add more water.

1. Put the corned beef brisket, fat-side up, in the bottom of the pressure cooker pot. Pour the contents of the seasoning packet over the top of the brisket, then add the water to the pot.

2. Close and lock the pressure cooker lid, make sure the pressure/steam-release switch is set to sealing, and set the cooking time to 1 hour 30 minutes at high/normal pressure (if using an electric pressure cooker; for stovetop pressure cookers, heat over a burner on high heat, set a timer for 1 hour 30 minutes after the pot has reached pressure, then reduce the heat to low). It will take about 14 minutes for the pot to come to pressure before the cooking time begins.

3. After the pressure cooking time ends, electric pressure cookers will automatically turn off their heat (stovetop pressure cookers must be removed from the heat). Release the pressure using the manufacturer's quick-release method.

4. Open the lid and transfer the corned beef to a large bowl. Pour the liquid from the pot into a large measuring cup until you have 1½ cups; pour the remaining liquid over the corned beef in the bowl.

LEFTOVER TIP

Leftover corned beef brisket is great for making a Reuben or plain corned beef sandwiches.

5. Pour the reserved 1½ cups of liquid back into the pressure cooker pot and place a steamer rack trivet in the bottom of the pot.

6. Put the cabbage, potatoes, and carrots on the trivet.

7. Close, lock, and seal the lid again, and set the cooking time to 4 minutes at high/normal pressure (if using an electric pressure cooker; for stovetop pressure cookers, heat over a burner on high heat, set a timer for 4 minutes after the pot has reached pressure, then reduce the heat to low). It will take about 15 minutes for the pot to reach pressure the second time.

8. After the pressure cooking time ends, electric pressure cookers will automatically turn off their heat (stovetop pressure cookers must be removed from the heat). Release the pressure using the manufacturer's quick-release method again.

9. Remove the corned beef from the bowl and carve, discarding the liquid. Serve it with the cabbage, potatoes, and carrots.

PER SERVING: Calories: 397; Total fat: 17g; Saturated Fat: 7g; Cholesterol: 149mg; Sodium: 1815mg; Carbohydrates: 26g; Fiber: 5g; Protein: 41g

Stuffed Bell Peppers

30 MINUTES • GLUTEN-FREE • NUT-FREE • SERVES 4

PREP TIME: 10 minutes

TOTAL COOK TIME:
25 minutes

APPROX. PRESSURE BUILD:
7 minutes

PRESSURE COOK: 10 minutes

PRESSURE RELEASE:
5 minutes

1 cup water

4 medium green
bell peppers

1 pound ground beef

½ cup cooked white rice

¼ cup finely chopped onion

1 teaspoon dried oregano

½ teaspoon salt

¼ teaspoon freshly ground
black pepper

¼ teaspoon garlic powder

1 (8-ounce) can
tomato sauce

½ cup shredded
cheddar cheese

Meat, cheese, and vegetables cook together in this all-in-one meal that is done in fewer than 30 minutes. My family eats these stuffed bell peppers as a complete dinner, but you can serve them with a side salad, a cup of tomato soup, or some extra cooked rice on the side.

1. Pour the water into the pressure cooker pot and place a steamer rack trivet in the bottom.
2. Slice the tops off the bell peppers and remove the seeds and ribs.
3. In a medium bowl, mix the ground beef, rice, onion, oregano, salt, pepper, and garlic powder. Stuff the mixture inside the four peppers, being careful not to pack the filling down too hard and leaving some room at the top.
4. Stand the peppers on the trivet inside the pot. Pour some tomato sauce on top of each pepper, but don't let it overflow. You may not need to use all the tomato sauce.
5. Close and lock the pressure cooker lid, make sure the pressure/steam-release switch is set to sealing, and set the cooking time to 10 minutes at high/normal pressure (if using an electric pressure cooker; for stovetop pressure cookers, heat over a burner on high heat, set a timer for 10 minutes after the pot has reached pressure, then reduce the heat to low). It will take about 7 minutes for the pot to come to pressure with an electric pressure cooker (stovetop pressure cookers may reach pressure sooner).

6. After the pressure cooking time ends, electric pressure cookers will automatically turn off their heat (stovetop pressure cookers must be removed from the heat). Allow the pressure to release from the pot naturally for 5 minutes before releasing the remaining pressure using the manufacturer's quick-release method.

7. Open the lid and divide the shredded cheese over the top of the peppers. Close the lid again (it doesn't need to be locked or set to sealing) and leave the lid on for 1 to 2 minutes to melt the cheese over the top of the peppers.

8. Remove the bell peppers carefully with tongs.

PER SERVING: Calories: 304; Total Fat: 13g; Saturated Fat: 6g; Cholesterol: 85mg; Sodium: 734mg; Carbohydrates: 20g; Fiber: 3g; Protein: 28g

INGREDIENT TIP

You may have enough filling for five peppers with this recipe. If you can fit a fifth pepper in your pressure cooker pot, you can get an extra serving with this recipe without any additional ingredients or cooking time.

Fall-off-the-Bone Pork Ribs

DAIRY-FREE • GLUTEN-FREE • KETO • NUT-FREE • SERVES 2 TO 4

PREP TIME: 5 minutes

TOTAL COOK TIME:
50 minutes

APPROX. PRESSURE BUILD:
11 minutes

PRESSURE COOK:
25 minutes

PRESSURE RELEASE:
15 minutes

2 teaspoons salt

1 teaspoon paprika

½ teaspoon dried thyme

½ teaspoon garlic powder

½ teaspoon onion powder

½ teaspoon ground
white pepper

½ teaspoon
cayenne pepper

¼ teaspoon freshly ground
black pepper

1 (2-pound) rack baby back
pork ribs

1 cup chicken broth,
store-bought or homemade
(page 170)

2 tablespoons apple
cider vinegar

These ribs are effortless to make and so tender that they live up to their name. You can serve them for a party or as a dinner entrée. The homemade seasoning rub provides enough flavor on its own, but you can also slather some of your favorite barbecue sauce on the ribs after they are done cooking.

1. In a small bowl, mix the salt, paprika, thyme, garlic powder, onion powder, white pepper, cayenne pepper, and black pepper. Rub this spice mixture all over the ribs.

2. Pour the chicken broth and apple cider vinegar into the pressure cooker pot, stirring to combine.

3. Place a steamer rack trivet in the bottom of the pot, and place the ribs on the trivet, standing the rack on its side, meaty-side out, and wrapping it around the inside of the pot into a circle or semicircle.

4. Close and lock the pressure cooker lid, make sure the pressure/steam-release switch is set to sealing, and set the cooking time to 25 minutes at high/normal pressure (if using an electric pressure cooker; for stovetop pressure cookers, heat over a burner on high heat, set a timer for 25 minutes after the pot has reached pressure, then reduce the heat to low). It will take about 11 minutes for the pot to come to pressure before the cooking time begins.

5. After the pressure cooking time ends, electric pressure cookers will automatically turn off their heat (stovetop pressure cookers must be removed from the heat). Allow the pressure to release from the pot naturally for 15 minutes before releasing the remaining pressure using the manufacturer's quick-release method.

6. Remove the ribs from the pot and carve between the rib bones to serve.

PER SERVING: Calories: 416; Total Fat: 30g; Saturated Fat: 10g; Cholesterol: 96mg; Sodium: 1543mg; Carbohydrates: 1g; Fiber: 0g; Protein: 42g

Pulled Pork Sliders

DAIRY-FREE • NUT-FREE • SERVES 8

PREP TIME: 5 minutes	
TOTAL COOK TIME: 1 hour 40 minutes	
APPROX. PRESSURE BUILD: 7 to 8 minutes	
PRESSURE COOK: 1 hour	
PRESSURE RELEASE: 20 minutes	

4 pounds pork butt or pork shoulder, cut into 4 equal pieces

4 garlic cloves, halved lengthwise

2 teaspoons salt

1 teaspoon freshly ground black pepper

½ teaspoon onion powder

½ teaspoon paprika

1½ tablespoons vegetable oil

1 cup chicken broth, store-bought or homemade (page 170)

2 cups barbecue sauce, divided

Slider buns, for serving

This cookout favorite is often made in a slow cooker, but the time can be cut down significantly by making it in the pressure cooker; you don't have to heat up your kitchen for hours, but the pork still turns out impossibly tender. Serve the pulled pork with slider buns for a party or a cookout, allowing guests to build their own sliders.

1. Cut two deep slashes in each piece of pork. Stuff a piece of garlic into each slash.
2. In a small bowl, mix the salt, pepper, onion powder, and paprika. Rub this seasoning mixture all over the pork.
3. Select the sauté function on the pressure cooker (if using an electric pressure cooker; for stovetop pressure cookers, heat over a burner on medium-high heat). Heat the vegetable oil in the pot.
4. Add the pork to the pot (you may need to do this in batches) and cook for 2 minutes on each of the two largest sides, or until browned. Transfer the pork to a plate.
5. Add the chicken broth to the pot and scrape the bottom of the pot with a wooden spoon to loosen any browned bits. Stir in ½ cup of barbecue sauce. Press cancel or turn off the burner. Return the pork to the pot.
6. Close and lock the pressure cooker lid, make sure the pressure/steam-release switch is set to sealing, and set the cooking time to 1 hour at high/normal pressure (if using an electric pressure cooker; for stovetop pressure cookers, heat over a burner on high heat, set a timer for 1 hour after the pot has reached pressure, then reduce the heat to low). It will take 7 to 8 minutes for the pot to come to pressure before the cooking time begins.

INGREDIENT TIP

You can use your favorite flavor of barbecue sauce for these. I prefer my Chipotle Barbecue Sauce (page 176) with this recipe because I like the sweetness mixed with the slightly spicy and smoky chipotle.

7. After the pressure cooking time ends, electric pressure cookers will automatically turn off their heat (stovetop pressure cookers must be removed from the heat). Allow the pressure to release from the pot naturally for 20 minutes before releasing the remaining pressure using the manufacturer's quick-release method.

8. Transfer the pork to a large bowl, along with ½ cup of the liquid from the pressure cooker. Discard the remaining liquid in the pressure cooker pot. Using two forks, shred the pork. Mix in the remaining 1½ cups of barbecue sauce.

9. Serve scoops of the sauced pork on slider buns.

PER SERVING: Calories: 557; Total Fat: 18g; Saturated Fat: 4g; Cholesterol: 148mg; Sodium: 1848mg; Carbohydrates: 52g; Fiber: 2g; Protein: 48g

LEFTOVER TIP

Leftover meat can be saved for salads, tacos, rice and beans, or scrambled eggs.

Pork Chops with Scalloped Potatoes

NUT-FREE • SERVES 4

PREP TIME: 10 minutes

TOTAL COOK TIME:
55 minutes

APPROX. PRESSURE BUILD:
6 minutes plus 3 minutes

PRESSURE COOK:
25 minutes plus 10 minutes

PRESSURE RELEASE:
5 minutes

1 cup heavy cream

1 cup chicken broth,
store-bought or homemade
(page 170)

2 tablespoons
all-purpose flour

1 teaspoon salt, plus more
for seasoning

½ teaspoon freshly ground
black pepper, plus more for
seasoning

½ teaspoon garlic powder,
plus more for seasoning

2 pounds potatoes,
peeled and cut as thinly
as possible (¼ inch or
less), preferably using a
mandoline slicer

1½ cups shredded cheddar
cheese, divided

1½ cups water

1 pound boneless
pork chops

Your meat entrée and side dish are all prepared in the same pot for this easy dinner recipe. Some recipes will call for preparing the scalloped potatoes directly in the pressure cooker pot, but I prefer the pot-in-pot method as it allows me to make a thicker, creamier sauce for the potatoes without risk of getting my electric pressure cooker's burn notice.

1. In a medium bowl, whisk together the heavy cream, chicken broth, flour, 1 teaspoon of the salt, ½ teaspoon of pepper, and ½ teaspoon of garlic powder.

2. Layer half of the sliced potatoes in the bottom of a heat-safe bowl (I use a 7-cup glass bowl). Pour half of the cream mixture over the potatoes, then top with half of the shredded cheese. Repeat with another layer of potatoes, cream mixture, and cheese.

3. Pour the water into the pressure cooker pot and place a steamer rack trivet in the bottom. Place the bowl with the potatoes on the trivet.

4. Close and lock the pressure cooker lid, make sure the pressure/steam-release switch is set to sealing, and set the cooking time to 25 minutes at high/normal pressure (if using an electric pressure cooker; for stovetop pressure cookers, heat over a burner on high heat, set a timer for 25 minutes after the pot has reached pressure, then reduce the heat to low). It will take about 6 minutes for the pot to come to pressure before the cooking time begins.

COOKING TIPS

* A mandoline slicer is a helpful tool to ensure the potatoes are sliced into even slices. If they are different thicknesses, they may not cook at the same rate and you may end up with some firm potatoes. Always use a safety guard when using a mandoline slicer.

* If you find that your potatoes are still firm after the pork cooks, remove the pork and pressure cook the potatoes for an additional 5 minutes with a quick release.

* See the Cooking Tip on page 29 for how to use a bakeware sling.

5. After the pressure cooking time ends, electric pressure cookers will automatically turn off their heat (stovetop pressure cookers must be removed from the heat). Release the pressure using the manufacturer's quick-release method.

6. Open the lid and place a piece of aluminum foil over the potatoes (it doesn't need to be wrapped around the dish, just placed on top so that the bowl is covered completely).

7. Season both sides of the pork chops with salt, pepper, and garlic powder and place them on the foil that is over the potatoes.

8. Close, lock, and seal the lid again, and set the cooking time to 10 minutes at high/normal pressure (if using an electric pressure cooker; for stovetop pressure cookers, heat over a burner on high heat, set a timer for 10 minutes after the pot has reached pressure, then reduce the heat to low). It will take about 3 minutes for the pot to reach pressure the second time.

9. Allow the pressure to release from the pot naturally for 5 minutes before releasing the remaining pressure using the manufacturer's quick-release method again.

10. Remove the pork and foil and set aside. Remove the bowl with the potatoes from the pressure cooker pot and stir. Let the potatoes sit for 5 minutes to allow the sauce to thicken. Serve with the pork chops.

PER SERVING: Calories: 776; Total Fat: 56g; Saturated Fat: 29g; Cholesterol: 197mg; Sodium: 821mg; Carbohydrates: 41g; Fiber: 6g; Protein: 36g

Rosemary-Crusted Rack of Lamb

30 MINUTES • DAIRY-FREE • GLUTEN-FREE • KETO • NUT-FREE • SERVES 2 TO 4

PREP TIME: 5 minutes

TOTAL COOK TIME: 25 minutes

APPROX. PRESSURE BUILD: 5 minutes

PRESSURE COOK: 2 minutes

PRESSURE RELEASE: 10 minutes

4 garlic cloves, minced

1 tablespoon dried rosemary

½ teaspoon salt

½ teaspoon freshly ground black pepper

1 pound lamb rack (4 to 6 ribs), cut in half

1 tablespoon olive oil

¼ cup dry red wine

¾ cup beef broth

This meal is perfect for a special occasion or at-home date night—think a cozy Valentine's Day dinner for two. Serve the rack of lamb with some polenta and sautéed mixed vegetables like green beans, colorful bell peppers, and onions for a stunning but easy home-cooked meal.

1. In a small bowl, mix the minced garlic, rosemary, salt, and pepper. Rub this mixture all over the meaty part of the ribs.
2. Select the sauté function on the pressure cooker (if using an electric pressure cooker; for stovetop pressure cookers, heat over a burner on medium-high heat). Heat the olive oil in the pot.
3. Add the lamb rack pieces to the pot and sauté for 2 minutes per side, or until brown (you might need to work in two batches). Transfer the lamb to a plate.
4. Pour the red wine into the pot, scraping the bottom of the pot with a wooden spoon to loosen any browned bits. Stir in the beef broth.
5. Place a steamer rack trivet in the bottom of the pot and place the lamb racks on the trivet, standing them up with meat-side down and the bone-side up. Prop the rib bones of the two pieces together to help them stand like a triangle.

6. Close and lock the pressure cooker lid, make sure the pressure/steam-release switch is set to sealing, and set the cooking time to 2 minutes at high/normal pressure (if using an electric pressure cooker; for stovetop pressure cookers, heat over a burner on high heat, set a timer for 2 minutes after the pot has reached pressure, then reduce the heat to low). It will take about 5 minutes for the pot to come to pressure before the cooking time begins.

7. After the pressure cooking time ends, electric pressure cookers will automatically turn off their heat (stovetop pressure cookers must be removed from the heat). Allow the pressure to release from the pot naturally for 10 minutes before releasing the remaining pressure using the manufacturer's quick-release method.

8. Remove the lamb from the pot and allow it to rest for 5 minutes before carving between the bones.

PER SERVING: Calories: 495; Total Fat: 28g; Saturated Fat: 8g; Cholesterol: 150mg; Sodium: 931mg; Carbohydrates: 5g; Fiber: 1g; Protein: 48g

COOKING TIP

Lamb is usually served rare to medium-rare. If you prefer yours more on the rare side, reduce the pressure cooking time to 1 minute. If you prefer it more on the medium side, increase the time to 3 or 4 minutes.

9

BEANS, RICE, PASTA, *and* GRAINS

Puerto Rican–Style Beans

DAIRY-FREE • GLUTEN-FREE • NUT-FREE • SERVES 6

PREP TIME: 10 minutes

TOTAL COOK TIME:
35 minutes

APPROX. PRESSURE BUILD:
13 minutes

PRESSURE COOK: 15 minutes

PRESSURE RELEASE:
2 minutes

1 tablespoon olive oil

4 ounces salt pork or ham, cut into ½-inch cubes

½ cup Goya Recaito (see tip)

1 teaspoon ground cumin

1 packet Goya Sazón con Culantro y Achiote (see tip)

1¾ cups chicken broth, store-bought or homemade (page 170)

2 (15.5-ounce) cans pink beans or kidney beans, rinsed and drained

1 (8-ounce) can tomato sauce

⅓ cup Spanish-style green olives stuffed with pimentos

1 tablespoon capers

¼ teaspoon salt (optional)

¼ teaspoon freshly ground black pepper

2 large potatoes, peeled and cut into 1-inch pieces

This Puerto Rican dish is an adaptation of my dad's recipe for habichuelas guisadas *(stewed beans). It is one of my husband's favorite things that I cook, and with the pressure cooker it is done in about half the time and with much less effort and monitoring. This can be eaten as an entrée on its own, but we usually serve it as an accompaniment to arroz con pollo. If you plan to serve this as an entrée, you may want to double the amount of salt pork for additional protein.*

1. Select the sauté function on the pressure cooker (if using an electric pressure cooker; for stovetop pressure cookers, heat over a burner on medium-high heat). Heat the olive oil in the pot.

2. Add the salt pork and sauté for 2 minutes. Add the Goya Recaito, cumin, and Sazón seasoning and sauté for 2 minutes. Press cancel or turn off the burner.

3. Stir in the chicken broth, scraping the bottom of the pot to loosen any browned bits. Add the beans, tomato sauce, olives, capers, salt (if using), and pepper and stir well to combine. Stir the potatoes into the bean mixture.

4. Close and lock the pressure cooker lid, make sure the pressure/steam-release switch is set to sealing, and set the cooking time to 15 minutes at high/normal pressure (if using an electric pressure cooker; for stovetop pressure cookers, heat over a burner on high heat, set a timer for 15 minutes after the pot has reached pressure, then reduce the heat to low). It will take about 13 minutes for the pot to come to pressure before the cooking time begins.

5. After the pressure cooking time ends, electric pressure cookers will automatically turn off their heat (stovetop pressure cookers must be removed from the heat). Release the pressure using the manufacturer's quick-release method.

6. Open the lid and stir the contents. The sauce will thicken as it stands.

PER SERVING: Calories: 284; Total Fat: 10g; Saturated Fat: 2g; Cholesterol: 10mg; Sodium: 1561mg; Carbohydrates: 37g; Fiber: 9g; Protein: 13g

INGREDIENT TIPS

* Instead of Goya Recaito, you can make your own sofrito for this dish. Simply purée 1 yellow onion, 2 whole heads of garlic (peeled), 2 teaspoons dried oregano, 1 green bell pepper (seeded), and 1 bunch fresh *culantro* or *ngo gai* (if you can find it; if not just use regular cilantro). I freeze my homemade sofrito in ½-cup portions to use whenever I'm making a savory Puerto Rican recipe. Note that Goya also makes a product called Sofrito, but their Recaito works better in this recipe.

* This meal gets its lovely yellow color from the achiote (annatto) in the Goya Sazón con Culantro y Achiote seasoning packet. Goya makes a few varieties of Sazón, so make sure not to buy the one labeled "Sazón sin Achiote"—that means it does not have achiote!

Easiest Spanish-Style Rice

30 MINUTES · DAIRY-FREE · GLUTEN-FREE · NUT-FREE · SERVES 6

PREP TIME: 5 minutes

TOTAL COOK TIME:
25 minutes

APPROX. PRESSURE BUILD:
6 minutes

PRESSURE COOK: 3 minutes

PRESSURE RELEASE:
10 minutes

2 tablespoons vegetable oil

2 tablespoons finely chopped onion

2 cups long-grain white rice, rinsed until the water runs clear

1½ cups chicken broth, store-bought or homemade (page 170)

1 (10-ounce) can diced tomatoes with green chiles (such as Ro-Tel)

1 teaspoon seasoning salt

½ teaspoon chili powder

¼ teaspoon garlic powder

This super simple rice recipe is a staple in our house. I love that just a few additional ingredients can turn your rice into something restaurant-worthy to serve alongside Mexican dishes like enchiladas, tacos, chiles rellenos, and more.

1. Select the sauté function on the pressure cooker (if using an electric pressure cooker; for stovetop pressure cookers, heat over a burner on medium-high heat). Heat the vegetable oil in the pot.
2. Add the onion to the pot and sauté until soft, 1 to 2 minutes.
3. Stir in the rice and sauté for 2 minutes more. Press cancel or turn off the burner.
4. Stir in the chicken broth, diced tomatoes with green chiles with their juices, seasoning salt, chili powder, and garlic powder.
5. Close and lock the pressure cooker lid, make sure the pressure/steam-release switch is set to sealing, and set the cooking time to 3 minutes at high/normal pressure (if using an electric pressure cooker; for stovetop pressure cookers, heat over a burner on high heat, set a timer for 3 minutes after the pot has reached pressure, then reduce the heat to low). It will take about 6 minutes for the pot to come to pressure before the cooking time begins.

6. After the pressure cooking time ends, electric pressure cookers will automatically turn off their heat (stovetop pressure cookers must be removed from the heat). Allow the pressure to release from the pot naturally for 10 minutes before releasing the remaining pressure using the manufacturer's quick-release method.

7. Open the lid, fluff the rice with a fork, and serve.

PER SERVING: Calories: 283; Total Fat: 9g; Saturated Fat: 1g; Cholesterol: 6mg; Sodium: 615mg; Carbohydrates: 52g; Fiber: 1g; Protein: 6g

INGREDIENT TIP

You can use a jar of your favorite picante sauce in place of the diced tomatoes with green chiles.

3-Cheese Risotto

30 MINUTES • GLUTEN-FREE • NUT-FREE • SERVES 6

PREP TIME: 10 minutes
TOTAL COOK TIME: 30 minutes
APPROX. PRESSURE BUILD: 10 to 11 minutes
PRESSURE COOK: 6 minutes
PRESSURE RELEASE: 1 minute

3 tablespoons unsalted butter

1 cup finely chopped onion

2 garlic cloves, minced

1½ cups arborio rice

½ cup dry white wine

3 cups chicken broth, store-bought or homemade (page 170)

1 cup heavy cream

½ teaspoon salt

¼ teaspoon freshly ground black pepper

½ cup shredded fontina cheese

½ cup shredded mozzarella cheese

½ cup shredded Parmesan cheese

If you've been too intimidated to try making homemade risotto, have no fear! This easy pressure-cooker recipe makes creamy risotto with a shockingly low amount of effort on your part. Start with the ingredients suggested here, then feel free to experiment with different cheeses (Asiago and Romano are great choices) or by adding sliced vegetables or mushrooms.

1. Select the sauté function on the pressure cooker (if using an electric pressure cooker; for stovetop pressure cookers, heat over a burner on medium-high heat). Melt the butter in the pot.

2. Add the onion and garlic and sauté for 2 minutes.

3. Add the rice and wine and stir well. Sauté for 2½ minutes, then stir in the chicken broth, heavy cream, salt, and pepper. Press cancel or turn off the burner.

4. Close and lock the pressure cooker lid, make sure the pressure/steam-release switch is set to sealing, and set the cooking time to 6 minutes at high/normal pressure (if using an electric pressure cooker; for stovetop pressure cookers, heat over a burner on high heat, set a timer for 6 minutes after the pot has reached pressure, then reduce the heat to low). It will take 10 to 11 minutes for the pot to come to pressure before the cooking time begins.

5. After the pressure cooking time ends, electric pressure cookers will automatically turn off their heat (stovetop pressure cookers must be removed from the heat). Release the pressure using the manufacturer's quick-release method.
6. Open the lid and gradually stir in the cheeses until they are melted.
7. Let the risotto sit in the pot, uncovered, until thickened, 3 to 4 minutes, then serve.

PER SERVING: Calories: 464; Total Fat: 35g; Saturated Fat: 17g; Cholesterol: 104mg; Sodium: 539mg; Carbohydrates: 43g; Fiber: 2g; Protein: 14g

INGREDIENT TIP

For a lighter variation, you can substitute an additional cup of broth in place of the heavy cream.

Chicken Penne Pasta with Vodka Sauce

30 MINUTES • NUT-FREE • SERVES 8

PREP TIME: 5 minutes

TOTAL COOK TIME:
30 minutes

APPROX. PRESSURE BUILD:
12 minutes

PRESSURE COOK: 5 minutes

PRESSURE RELEASE:
3 minutes

In this dish, the pasta cooks together with the chicken and sauce in one pot. It makes enough to serve a crowd, or you can save the leftovers for lunches to eat over the following few days. This recipe was written for a 6- or 8-quart pressure cooker; if you are using a smaller pressure cooker, you should halve the recipe—the timing remains the same.

2 tablespoons
unsalted butter

1 to 1½ pounds boneless,
skinless chicken breasts,
cut into bite-size pieces

1 medium onion,
finely chopped

3 garlic cloves, minced

½ cup vodka

1 pound uncooked
penne pasta

1 (28-ounce) can
tomato purée

3 cups water

1 teaspoon salt

½ teaspoon freshly ground
black pepper

¼ teaspoon garlic powder

½ cup heavy cream

¼ cup grated
Romano cheese

Grated Parmesan cheese,
for garnish

Chopped fresh parsley,
for garnish

1. Select the sauté function on the pressure cooker (if using an electric pressure cooker; for stovetop pressure cookers, heat over a burner on medium-high heat). Melt the butter in the pot.

2. Add the chicken and onion and sauté until the chicken is browned, about 6 minutes. Add the garlic and sauté for 1 minute more.

3. Add the vodka to the pot and stir well. Sauté for 2 minutes, then press cancel or turn off the burner.

4. Stir in the pasta, tomato purée, water, salt, pepper, and garlic powder.

5. Close and lock the pressure cooker lid, make sure the pressure/steam-release switch is set to sealing, and set the cooking time to 5 minutes at high/normal pressure (if using an electric pressure cooker; for stovetop pressure cookers, heat over a burner on high heat, set a timer for 5 minutes after the pot has reached pressure, then reduce the heat to low). It will take about 12 minutes for the pot to come to pressure before the cooking time begins.

6. After the pressure cooking time ends, electric pressure cookers will automatically turn off their heat (stovetop pressure cookers must be removed from the heat). Release the pressure using the manufacturer's quick-release method.

7. Open the lid and stir in the heavy cream and Romano cheese. Let the pasta sit in the pot until the sauce is thickened, about 3 minutes. Garnish with Parmesan cheese and parsley.

PER SERVING: Calories: 339; Total Fat: 12g; Saturated Fat: 6g; Cholesterol: 67mg; Sodium: 458mg; Carbohydrates: 32g; Fiber: 3g; Protein: 21g

Hearty Beef and Bean Pasta

30 MINUTES · NUT-FREE · SERVES 8

PREP TIME: 5 minutes

TOTAL COOK TIME:
30 minutes

APPROX. PRESSURE BUILD:
16 minutes

PRESSURE COOK: 5 minutes

PRESSURE RELEASE:
2 minutes

2 tablespoons olive oil

1 pound chuck or flank
steak, cut into thin strips

1½ cups chopped onion

3 cups beef broth

1 (28-ounce) can diced
tomatoes

1 (15-ounce) can kidney
beans, rinsed and drained

1 (8-ounce) can
tomato sauce

1 teaspoon paprika

1 teaspoon ground cumin

1 teaspoon dried thyme

1 teaspoon salt

½ teaspoon freshly
ground pepper

½ teaspoon garlic powder

½ teaspoon onion powder

1 pound uncooked
rotini pasta

½ cup shredded
cheddar cheese

*I love making this large-batch pasta dish to freeze
into portions then reheat later on busy nights. It is
also a thoughtful gift for parents with a new baby at
home who might be too tired to cook for themselves.
This recipe was written for a 6- or 8-quart pressure
cooker; if you are using a smaller pressure cooker, you
should halve the recipe—the timing remains the same.*

1. Select the sauté function on the pressure cooker (if
   using an electric pressure cooker; for stovetop pressure
   cookers, heat over a burner on medium-high heat). Heat
   the olive oil in the pot.

2. Add the steak and onion and sauté until the meat is
   browned, about 5 minutes.

3. Pour the beef broth into the pot and scrape the bottom
   of the pot with a spoon to loosen any browned bits.
   Press cancel or turn off the burner.

4. Stir in the diced tomatoes with their juices, kidney
   beans, tomato sauce, paprika, cumin, thyme, salt,
   pepper, garlic powder, and onion powder until well
   mixed. Stir in the pasta, mixing well so that the pasta is
   mostly submerged in the liquid.

5. Close and lock the pressure cooker lid, make sure the
   pressure/steam-release switch is set to sealing, and
   set the cooking time to 5 minutes at high/normal pressure (if using an electric pressure cooker; for stovetop
   pressure cookers, heat over a burner on high heat, set
   a timer for 5 minutes after the pot has reached pressure, then reduce the heat to low). It will take about
   16 minutes for the pot to come to pressure before the
   cooking time begins.

6. After the pressure cooking time ends, electric pressure cookers will automatically turn off their heat (stovetop pressure cookers must be removed from the heat). Release the pressure using the manufacturer's quick-release method.

7. Open the lid and stir the pasta. Top with the shredded cheddar cheese.

PER SERVING: Calories: 326; Total Fat: 9g; Saturated Fat: 2g; Cholesterol: 7mg; Sodium: 675mg; Carbohydrates: 38g; Fiber: 6g; Protein: 25g

HOW TO STORE AND FREEZE

This recipe freezes and reheats well. Here are steps to freeze and store half the leftovers to serve another day.

* Before topping with the cheese, transfer half of the pasta mixture to an 8-inch baking dish lined with aluminum foil, with extra foil hanging over the sides. When it has cooled a bit, move it to the refrigerator to chill until most of the heat is gone.

* Transfer the baking dish to the freezer and cool until set and firm but not frozen. This allows the food to retain the shape of the baking dish for storage.

* Remove the foil with the pasta from the baking dish and wrap the excess foil around the food. Wrap the pasta a few times with more foil so that no food it exposed.

* Place the wrapped food in a gallon-size plastic freezer bag and remove as much of the air as possible before sealing.

* Store in the freezer, then transfer to the refrigerator to defrost the night before you plan to reheat and serve it again.

* When ready to reheat, preheat the oven to 350°F. Unwrap the pasta from the foil and place it back in its 8-inch baking dish. Top with shredded cheddar cheese and heat until warmed through.

White Cheddar Mac and Cheese with Pesto and Bacon

30 MINUTES • NUT-FREE • SERVES 8

PREP TIME: 5 minutes

TOTAL COOK TIME: 20 minutes

APPROX. PRESSURE BUILD: 9 to 10 minutes

PRESSURE COOK: 6 minutes

PRESSURE RELEASE: 2 minutes

1 pound uncooked elbow macaroni

2 cups chicken broth, store-bought or homemade (page 170)

2 cups water

3 garlic cloves, minced

1 teaspoon salt

½ teaspoon freshly ground black pepper

¾ cup milk

2 cups shredded white cheddar cheese

1 cup shredded Parmesan cheese

¼ cup basil pesto

½ cup real bacon bits

This upgraded macaroni and cheese is a great side dish for a holiday meal—though you might find that it is the star of the meal! It cooks really quickly in the pressure cooker, so it won't take effort away from other food you're cooking.

1. Stir together the macaroni, chicken broth, water, garlic, salt, and pepper in the pressure cooker pot.

2. Close and lock the pressure cooker lid, make sure the pressure/steam-release switch is set to sealing, and set the cooking time to 6 minutes at high/normal pressure (if using an electric pressure cooker; for stovetop pressure cookers, heat over a burner on high heat, set a timer for 6 minutes after the pot has reached pressure, then reduce the heat to low). It will take 9 to 10 minutes for the pot to come to pressure before the cooking time begins.

3. After the pressure cooking time ends, electric pressure cookers will automatically turn off their heat (stovetop pressure cookers must be removed from the heat). Release the pressure using the manufacturer's quick-release method.

INGREDIENT TIP

I use real bacon bits as a time saver (the soft, meaty kind you find in pouches in the grocery store, not the hard, dehydrated kind in the bottle), but if you'd like to use fresh bacon, simply fry 6 strips of bacon, then crumble or chop them.

4. Open the lid and gradually stir in the milk and cheeses, alternating between a little of the milk and a handful of cheese at a time, and stir until the cheeses are melted. Stir in the pesto until well mixed. Finally, stir in the bacon.

PER SERVING: Calories: 311; Total Fat: 18g; Saturated Fat: 9g; Cholesterol: 53mg; Sodium: 860mg; Carbohydrates: 24g; Fiber: 1g; Protein: 20g

SERVING TIP

I recommend transferring the pasta to a serving dish for presentation purposes, garnished with some coarsely chopped fresh basil.

Everyday Pressure Cooker Lasagna

NUT-FREE • **SERVES 4 TO 6**

PREP TIME: 5 minutes
TOTAL COOK TIME: 1 hour
APPROX. PRESSURE BUILD: 4 minutes
PRESSURE COOK: 26 minutes
PRESSURE RELEASE: 10 minutes

1 pound ground
Italian sausage

1½ cups ricotta cheese

½ cup shredded Parmesan
cheese, divided

1 large egg, lightly beaten

1 teaspoon Italian
seasoning

½ teaspoon salt

¼ teaspoon freshly ground
black pepper

¼ teaspoon garlic powder

¼ teaspoon onion powder

1 (24-ounce) jar pasta
sauce, divided

6 oven-ready/no-boil
lasagna noodles

1 cup shredded
mozzarella cheese

1 cup water

Lasagna's size and complicated cooking method usually means you make the dish only for special occasions, but I call this "everyday" lasagna because it's hands-off enough for a weeknight dinner and portioned perfectly for a family of four. You can stretch it to six servings by serving it with a side salad.

1. Select the sauté function on the pressure cooker (if using an electric pressure cooker; for stovetop pressure cookers, heat over a burner on medium-high heat). Cook the ground sausage in the pot, crumbling the meat with a wooden spoon, until it is browned and cooked through, 8 to 10 minutes. Press cancel or turn off the burner, then transfer to a plate lined with paper towels to drain. When it's cool enough to handle, wipe out the pressure cooker pot.

2. In a medium bowl, mix together the ricotta cheese, ¼ cup of Parmesan cheese, egg, Italian seasoning, salt, pepper, garlic powder, and onion powder.

3. Line a springform pan (or other heat-safe dish) with aluminum foil (see tip). Spread ¼ cup of pasta sauce in the bottom of the springform pan. Mix the remaining pasta sauce with the cooked sausage in a small bowl.

4. Break 2 lasagna noodles into large pieces and scatter them evenly over the pasta sauce in the springform pan. Top with half of the ricotta mixture, spreading the mixture out evenly. Add half of the sausage mixture on top of the ricotta. Repeat with another layer of 2 noodles (broken), the remaining ricotta mixture, and the remaining sausage mixture.

COOKING TIPS

∗ You can use a foil-lined
7-inch springform pan or a
7-cup glass bowl to make
this recipe. The key is to
make sure whatever dish
or pan you use is at least
3 inches tall for the layers of
lasagna to fit inside it.

∗ See the Cooking Tip on
page 29 for how to use a
bakeware sling.

5. Break the last 2 lasagna noodles and scatter them
   evenly over the top. Top with the mozzarella cheese and
   remaining ¼ cup of Parmesan cheese. Cover the pan
   with aluminum foil.

6. Pour the water into the pressure cooker pot and place a
   steamer rack trivet in the bottom. Place the pan with the
   lasagna on the trivet.

7. Close and lock the pressure cooker lid, make sure the
   pressure/steam-release switch is set to sealing, and set
   the cooking time to 26 minutes at high/normal pressure (if using an electric pressure cooker; for stovetop
   pressure cookers, heat over a burner on high heat, set a
   timer for 26 minutes after the pot has reached pressure,
   then reduce the heat to low). It will take about 4 minutes
   for the pot to come to pressure before the cooking
   time begins.

8. After the pressure cooking time ends, electric pressure
   cookers will automatically turn off their heat (stovetop
   pressure cookers must be removed from the heat).
   Allow the pressure to release from the pot naturally
   for 10 minutes before releasing the remaining pressure
   using the manufacturer's quick-release method.

9. Open the lid and carefully remove the pot with the
   lasagna from the pressure cooker. Allow the lasagna to
   rest for 10 minutes before serving.

PER SERVING: Calories: 606; Total Fat: 30g; Saturated Fat: 13g;
Cholesterol: 133mg; Sodium: 1506mg; Carbohydrates: 49g; Fiber: 4g;
Protein: 32g

Cilantro-Lime Rice

30 MINUTES • DAIRY-FREE • GLUTEN-FREE • NUT-FREE • VEGAN • SERVES 4

PREP TIME: 5 minutes

TOTAL COOK TIME:
20 minutes

APPROX. PRESSURE BUILD:
5 minutes

PRESSURE COOK: 4 minutes

PRESSURE RELEASE:
10 minutes

1 cup long-grain white
rice, rinsed until the water
runs clear

1 cup water

½ teaspoon salt

1 tablespoon finely
chopped fresh cilantro

1 teaspoon grated lime zest

1 tablespoon fresh
lime juice

1 teaspoon vegetable oil

COOKING TIP

When making any rice dish in a
pressure cooker, it is important
to rinse the rice thoroughly
first. Removing excess starch
will help prevent foaming
while cooking. Foamy foods
can pose a safety concern
for pressure cookers, as the
froth can sometimes block the
pressure-release valves.

*Rice is unbelievably quick to make in a pressure
cooker and requires a lot less liquid than the
traditional method. This cilantro-lime rice is delicious
as a side dish or as an addition to a burrito or taco
bowl. Serve it with tacos or other Mexican fare and
some black beans.*

1. Combine the rice, water, and salt in the pressure cooker
   pot and stir.
2. Close and lock the pressure cooker lid, make sure the
   pressure/steam-release switch is set to sealing, and set
   the cooking time to 4 minutes at high/normal pressure
   (if using an electric pressure cooker; for stovetop pressure cookers, heat over a burner on high heat, set a
   timer for 4 minutes after the pot has reached pressure,
   then reduce the heat to low). It will take about 5 minutes
   for the pot to come to pressure before the cooking
   time begins.
3. After the pressure cooking time ends, electric pressure
   cookers will automatically turn off their heat (stovetop
   pressure cookers must be removed from the heat).
   Allow the pressure to release from the pot naturally
   for 10 minutes before releasing the remaining pressure
   using the manufacturer's quick-release method.
4. Open the lid and stir in the cilantro, lime zest and juice,
   and oil. Fluff with a fork and serve.

PER SERVING: Calories: 182; Total Fat: 2g; Saturated Fat: 0g;
Cholesterol: 0mg; Sodium: 293mg; Carbohydrates: 38g; Fiber: 1g;
Protein: 3g

10

STEWS, SOUPS, and CHILIS

Ratatouille

30 MINUTES • DAIRY-FREE • GLUTEN-FREE • NUT-FREE • VEGAN • SERVES 4

PREP TIME: 10 minutes

TOTAL COOK TIME:
25 minutes

APPROX. PRESSURE BUILD:
12 minutes

PRESSURE COOK: 6 minutes

PRESSURE RELEASE:
1 minute

4 tablespoons olive
oil, divided

1 medium eggplant,
quartered lengthwise and
then cut crosswise into
½-inch slices

1 medium onion, cut into
½-inch slices

1 large or 2 small zucchini,
cut into ½-inch slices

1 yellow bell pepper,
seeded and cut into
2-inch chunks

3 garlic cloves, chopped

1 (28-ounce) can whole
peeled tomatoes

1 teaspoon dried
summer savory

Coarse salt

Freshly ground
black pepper

I included this recipe for the classic Provençal French vegetable stew at the request of my sons, who love the movie by the same name. The flavors marry beautifully while it cooks quickly in the pressure cooker. This versatile dish can be served either as a comforting entrée or as a side dish.

1. Select the sauté function on the pressure cooker (if using an electric pressure cooker; for stovetop pressure cookers, heat over a burner on medium-high heat). Heat 2 tablespoons of olive oil in the pot.

2. Add the eggplant and onion and sauté, stirring occasionally, for 2 minutes.

3. Stir in the remaining 2 tablespoons of olive oil. Add the zucchini, bell pepper, and garlic and sauté for 2 minutes. Press cancel or turn off the burner.

4. Stir in the canned tomatoes with their juices, scraping the bottom of the pot to loosen any browned bits. Add the summer savory and season with salt and pepper. Stir until the seasonings are well mixed with the vegetables.

5. Close and lock the pressure cooker lid, make sure the pressure/steam-release switch is set to sealing, and set the cooking time to 6 minutes at high/normal pressure (if using an electric pressure cooker; for stovetop pressure cookers, heat over a burner on high heat, set a timer for 6 minutes after the pot has reached pressure, then reduce the heat to low). It will take about 12 minutes for the pot to come to pressure before the cooking time begins.

6. After the pressure cooking time ends, electric pressure cookers will automatically turn off their heat (stovetop pressure cookers must be removed from the heat). Release the pressure using the manufacturer's quick-release method.

7. Open the lid, season with additional salt and pepper as needed, and serve.

PER SERVING: Calories: 205; Total Fat: 13g; Saturated Fat: 2g; Cholesterol: 0mg; Sodium: 411mg; Carbohydrates: 21g; Fiber: 7g; Protein: 4g

INGREDIENT TIP

If you don't have summer savory, you can substitute dried sage, thyme, herbes de Provence, or a combination.

Puerto Rican–Style Chicken Stew

DAIRY-FREE • GLUTEN-FREE • NUT-FREE • SERVES 4 TO 6

PREP TIME: 10 minutes

TOTAL COOK TIME:
40 minutes

APPROX. PRESSURE BUILD:
11 minutes

PRESSURE COOK: 10 minutes

PRESSURE RELEASE:
5 minutes

¼ cup olive oil

4 to 6 bone-in, skin-on chicken breasts or thighs

½ cup dry white wine

3 tablespoons white vinegar

1 (8-ounce) can tomato sauce

1½ pounds potatoes, peeled and cut into 1-inch pieces

1 medium onion, chopped

¼ cup Spanish-style green olives stuffed with pimentos

6 garlic cloves, chopped

1 teaspoon capers

1½ teaspoons salt

I adapted this recipe for estofado de pollo *from one of my mother's specialties. It has a wonderful vinegary taste with a light red sauce. It can be made with chicken breasts or thighs or a combination of both. My family likes to eat it over white rice, but it can be enjoyed on its own.*

1. Select the sauté function on the pressure cooker (if using an electric pressure cooker; for stovetop pressure cookers, heat over a burner on medium-high heat). Heat the olive oil in the pot.

2. Add the chicken to the pot and cook for 4 minutes on each side. Transfer the chicken to a plate.

3. Add the wine and vinegar to the pot, scraping the bottom of the pot to loosen any browned bits. Cook, stirring occasionally, for 3 minutes. Press cancel or turn off the burner.

4. Add the tomato sauce to the pot and stir until well mixed. Stir in the potatoes, onion, olives, garlic, capers, and salt. Return the chicken to the pot and spoon some of the sauce over the top of the chicken.

5. Close and lock the pressure cooker lid, make sure the pressure/steam-release switch is set to sealing, and set the cooking time to 10 minutes at high/normal pressure (if using an electric pressure cooker; for stovetop pressure cookers, heat over a burner on high heat, set a timer for 10 minutes after the pot has reached pressure, then reduce the heat to low). It will take about 11 minutes for the pot to come to pressure before the cooking time begins.

6. After the pressure cooking time ends, electric pressure cookers will automatically turn off their heat (stovetop pressure cookers must be removed from the heat). Allow the pressure to release from the pot naturally for 5 minutes before releasing the remaining pressure using the manufacturer's quick-release method.

7. Open the lid and select the sauté function on the pot again. Simmer for 5 minutes, stirring occasionally, then press cancel or turn off the burner.

PER SERVING: Calories: 533; Total Fat: 20g; Saturated Fat: 4g; Cholesterol: 129mg; Sodium: 1347mg; Carbohydrates: 38g; Fiber: 6g; Protein: 46g

Irish Stout Beef Stew

DAIRY-FREE • NUT-FREE • SERVES 6

PREP TIME: 10 minutes

TOTAL COOK TIME: 1 hour 5 minutes

APPROX. PRESSURE BUILD: 15 minutes

PRESSURE COOK: 35 minutes

PRESSURE RELEASE: 10 minutes

1 tablespoon vegetable oil

2 pounds chuck roast, cut into bite-size pieces

2 cups beef broth

1 cup Irish stout beer (such as Guinness)

3 tablespoons tomato paste

1 tablespoon Worcestershire sauce

1½ teaspoons salt

1 teaspoon freshly ground black pepper

½ teaspoon garlic powder

1 pound potatoes, peeled and cut into 1-inch pieces

1 large onion, chopped

3 carrots, peeled and chopped into 2-inch pieces

Chopped fresh parsley, for garnish

One of my favorite food memories from traveling to Ireland was sitting in a medieval inn and enjoying the most comforting, rich, and hearty beef stew. I always think of stews when I think of Irish food, and my mind usually floats to the delicious stout that often accompanies one. This recipe is a combination of those two things: a hearty Irish-inspired stew flavored with a rich stout beer. Serve Irish soda bread or sourdough bread on the side.

1. Select the sauté function on the pressure cooker (if using an electric pressure cooker; for stovetop pressure cookers, heat over a burner on medium-high heat). Heat the oil in the pot.

2. Add the beef to the pot and sauté until browned on all sides, about 4 minutes. Press cancel or turn off the burner.

3. Add the beef broth and beer to the pot, scraping the bottom of the pot to loosen any browned bits.

4. Stir in the tomato paste, Worcestershire sauce, salt, pepper, and garlic powder until well mixed and no chunks of tomato paste are visible. Add the potatoes, onion, and carrots, stirring to combine.

5. Close and lock the pressure cooker lid, make sure the pressure/steam-release switch is set to sealing, and set the cooking time to 35 minutes at high/normal pressure (if using an electric pressure cooker; for stovetop pressure cookers, heat over a burner on high heat, set a timer for 35 minutes after the pot has reached pressure, then reduce the heat to low). It will take about 15 minutes for the pot to come to pressure before the cooking time begins.

6. After the pressure cooking time ends, electric pressure cookers will automatically turn off their heat (stovetop pressure cookers must be removed from the heat). Allow the pressure to release from the pot naturally for 10 minutes before releasing the remaining pressure using the manufacturer's quick-release method.

7. Open the lid and stir the stew, then garnish with fresh parsley.

PER SERVING: Calories: 386; Total Fat: 18g; Saturated Fat: 1g; Cholesterol: 2mg; Sodium: 833mg; Carbohydrates: 20g; Fiber: 4g; Protein: 33g

French Onion Soup

NUT-FREE · SERVES 6

PREP TIME: 5 minutes	
TOTAL COOK TIME: 55 minutes	
APPROX. PRESSURE BUILD: 12 to 13 minutes	
PRESSURE COOK: 10 minutes	
PRESSURE RELEASE: 10 minutes	

3 tablespoons unsalted butter

4 onions, thinly sliced

1 tablespoon sugar

1 cup dry red wine

1 teaspoon freshly ground black pepper

4 cups beef broth

2 cups water

1 teaspoon salt

½ teaspoon dried thyme

2 cups salad croutons

6 ounces Gruyère cheese, sliced

¼ cup grated Parmesan cheese

This soup is equally good as a comforting lunch on a cold day as it is a starter for a dinner with guests. The richness of the red wine and beef broth balance wonderfully with the lightly sweet caramelized onions.

1. Select the sauté function on the pressure cooker (if using an electric pressure cooker; for stovetop pressure cookers, heat over a burner on medium-high heat). Melt the butter in the pot.

2. Add the onions and sugar to the pot and sauté for 10 minutes, until the onions are starting to brown.

3. Add the wine and pepper, scraping the bottom of the pot to loosen any browned bits. Cook for 4 minutes.

4. Stir in the beef broth, water, salt, and thyme until well mixed. Press cancel or turn off the burner.

5. Close and lock the pressure cooker lid, make sure the pressure/steam-release switch is set to sealing, and set the cooking time to 10 minutes at high/normal pressure (if using an electric pressure cooker; for stovetop pressure cookers, heat over a burner on high heat, set a timer for 10 minutes after the pot has reached pressure, then reduce the heat to low). It will take 12 to 13 minutes for the pot to come to pressure before the cooking time begins.

6. After the pressure cooking time ends, electric pressure cookers will automatically turn off their heat (stovetop pressure cookers must be removed from the heat). Allow the pressure to release from the pot naturally for 10 minutes before releasing the remaining pressure using the manufacturer's quick-release method.

7. Open the lid and stir the soup. Add the croutons on the top of the soup in a single layer so that they are floating, then lay the slices of Gruyère cheese on top of the croutons (the croutons will keep the cheese from melting into the soup). Sprinkle the Parmesan cheese evenly on top of the Gruyère. Close the lid (no need to seal the lid, as you won't be cooking again) and leave it in place for 1 minute to melt the cheese with the pot's residual heat.

8. Ladle the soup into serving bowls, making sure to include some of the cheese and croutons in each.

PER SERVING: Calories: 304; Total Fat: 17g; Saturated Fat: 10g; Cholesterol: 50mg; Sodium: 908mg; Carbohydrates: 19g; Fiber: 2g; Protein: 13g

SERVING TIP

If you are serving this to guests and have the time, ladle the soup into crocks or other heat-safe bowls before adding the croutons and cheese. Place the crocks on a rimmed baking sheet, then add the croutons and cheeses to the tops of each bowl individually. Place under a broiler for 1 to 2 minutes to melt and lightly brown the cheese.

Comforting Chicken Noodle Soup

DAIRY-FREE • NUT-FREE • SERVES 4

PREP TIME: 10 minutes	
TOTAL COOK TIME: 40 minutes	
APPROX. PRESSURE BUILD: 15 to 16 minutes	
PRESSURE COOK: 10 minutes	
PRESSURE RELEASE: 3 minutes	

2 teaspoons vegetable oil

1 to 1½ pounds boneless, skinless chicken breasts, cut into 1-inch pieces

1 medium onion, chopped

2 carrots, peeled and chopped

2 celery stalks, chopped

4 cups water

3 cups chicken broth, store-bought or homemade (page 170)

½ teaspoon salt

¼ teaspoon freshly ground black pepper

¼ teaspoon garlic powder

2 cups uncooked egg noodles

2 tablespoons coarsely chopped fresh parsley

1 lemon, halved

My kids absolutely love this soup for lunch or dinner. And I always make it whenever someone in our family is under the weather, as there is nothing more comforting and healing than fresh chicken noodle soup. The tangy addition of lemon juice to finish the recipe is what makes this soup so crave-worthy.

1. Select the sauté function on the pressure cooker (if using an electric pressure cooker; for stovetop pressure cookers, heat over a burner on medium-high heat). Heat the oil in the pot.

2. Add the chicken, onion, carrots, and celery to the pot and sauté for 4 minutes. Press cancel or turn off the burner.

3. Add the water, chicken broth, salt, pepper, and garlic powder, scraping the bottom of the pot to loosen any browned bits, and stir until well mixed.

4. Close and lock the pressure cooker lid, make sure the pressure/steam-release switch is set to sealing, and set the cooking time to 10 minutes at high/normal pressure (if using an electric pressure cooker; for stovetop pressure cookers, heat over a burner on high heat, set a timer for 10 minutes after the pot has reached pressure, then reduce the heat to low). It will take 15 to 16 minutes for the pot to come to pressure before the cooking time begins.

5. After the pressure cooking time ends, electric pressure cookers will automatically turn off their heat (stovetop pressure cookers must be removed from the heat). Release the pressure using the manufacturer's quick-release method, about 3 minutes.

6. Open the lid, select the sauté function on the pot again, and stir in the egg noodles and parsley. Simmer until the noodles are cooked (about 7 to 8 minutes), then press cancel or turn off the burner. Squeeze the juice from the lemon halves into the soup and stir.

PER SERVING: Calories: 275; Total Fat: 17g; Saturated Fat: 1g; Cholesterol: 107mg; Sodium: 480mg; Carbohydrates: 20g; Fiber: 2g; Protein: 31g

Cuban Black Bean Soup

30 MINUTES • DAIRY-FREE • GLUTEN-FREE • NUT-FREE • VEGAN • SERVES 4

PREP TIME: 5 minutes

TOTAL COOK TIME:
30 minutes

APPROX. PRESSURE BUILD:
15 minutes

PRESSURE COOK: 10 minutes

PRESSURE RELEASE:
2 minutes

1 tablespoon olive oil

1 small onion,
coarsely chopped

1 green bell pepper, seeded
and coarsely chopped

4 garlic cloves, chopped

3 (14-ounce) cans black
beans, rinsed and drained

2 cups vegetable broth,
store-bought or homemade
(page 170)

2 teaspoons ground cumin

2 teaspoons dried oregano

1 teaspoon salt

½ teaspoon freshly ground
black pepper

1 tablespoon fresh
lime juice

¼ cup chopped fresh
cilantro

I love the combination of black beans and cumin, and both are key ingredients in this Cuban-style soup. This recipe is vegan and dairy-free, but you can add a dollop of sour cream (regular or dairy-free vegan sour cream) when serving for a tangy kick.

1. Select the sauté function on the pressure cooker (if using an electric pressure cooker; for stovetop pressure cookers, heat over a burner on medium-high heat). Heat the olive oil in the pot.

2. Add the onion, bell pepper, and garlic and sauté, stirring occasionally, for 4 minutes. Press cancel or turn off the burner.

3. While the onion mixture is sautéing, pour the black beans and vegetable broth into a food processor and pulse a few times until the beans are chopped but still a little chunky (you may need to work in batches depending on the size of your food processor).

4. Stir the bean mixture into the pot, scraping the bottom of the pot to loosen any browned bits. Add the cumin, oregano, salt, and pepper and stir well to combine.

5. Close and lock the pressure cooker lid, make sure the pressure/steam-release switch is set to sealing, and set the cooking time to 10 minutes at high/normal pressure (if using an electric pressure cooker; for stovetop pressure cookers, heat over a burner on high heat, set a timer for 10 minutes after the pot has reached pressure, then reduce the heat to low). It will take about 15 minutes for the pot to come to pressure before the cooking time begins.

6. After the pressure cooking time ends, electric pressure cookers will automatically turn off their heat (stovetop pressure cookers must be removed from the heat). Release the pressure using the manufacturer's quick-release method.

7. Open the lid and stir in the lime juice. Top each serving with cilantro.

PER SERVING: Calories: 334; Total Fat: 3g; Saturated Fat: 1g; Cholesterol: 0mg; Sodium: 734mg; Carbohydrates: 59g; Fiber: 20g; Protein: 20g

Classic Beef Chili

DAIRY-FREE · GLUTEN-FREE · NUT-FREE · SERVES 4

PREP TIME: 10 minutes

TOTAL COOK TIME:
45 minutes

APPROX. PRESSURE BUILD:
8 to 9 minutes

PRESSURE COOK: 15 minutes

PRESSURE RELEASE:
10 minutes

1 pound ground beef

1 green bell pepper, seeded
and finely chopped

1 medium onion,
finely chopped

3 garlic cloves, minced

1½ tablespoons
chili powder

2 teaspoons ground cumin

1 teaspoon salt

½ teaspoon freshly ground
black pepper

½ teaspoon paprika

¼ cup beef broth

2 tablespoons tomato paste

2 (14.5-ounce) cans diced
tomatoes

*This hearty, no-bean chili is great in a bowl topped
with shredded cheddar cheese, sour cream, and
chopped scallions or as a delicious topping for hot
dogs. My oldest son and husband love to add some
Tabasco sauce to their bowls to give it an extra kick.*

1. Select the sauté function on the pressure cooker (if
   using an electric pressure cooker; for stovetop pressure
   cookers, heat over a burner on medium-high heat). Add
   the ground beef, bell pepper, onion, garlic, chili powder,
   cumin, salt, pepper, and paprika and cook, stirring occasionally, until the meat is browned, about 10 minutes.

2. Add the beef broth to the pot, scraping the bottom of
   the pot to loosen any browned bits. Stir in the tomato
   paste. Press cancel or turn off the burner.

3. Add the diced tomatoes with their juices and stir until
   well mixed.

4. Close and lock the pressure cooker lid, make sure the
   pressure/steam-release switch is set to sealing, and set
   the cooking time to 15 minutes at high/normal pressure (if using an electric pressure cooker; for stovetop
   pressure cookers, heat over a burner on high heat, set a
   timer for 15 minutes after the pot has reached pressure,
   then reduce the heat to low). It will take 8 to 9 minutes
   for the pot to come to pressure before the cooking
   time begins.

5. After the pressure cooking time ends, electric pressure cookers will automatically turn off their heat (stovetop pressure cookers must be removed from the heat). Allow the pressure to release from the pot naturally for 10 minutes before releasing the remaining pressure using the manufacturer's quick-release method.

6. Open the lid and stir the chili.

PER SERVING: Calories: 244; Total Fat: 9g; Saturated Fat: 3g; Cholesterol: 70mg; Sodium: 765mg; Carbohydrates: 17g; Fiber: 5g; Protein: 26g

INGREDIENT TIP

If you prefer your chili with beans, you can add 2 (14-ounce) cans of kidney beans (rinsed and drained) before pressure cooking and increase the pressure cooking time to 18 minutes.

11

BROTHS
and SAUCES

Vegetable Broth

DAIRY-FREE • GLUTEN-FREE • NUT-FREE • VEGAN • MAKES ABOUT 10 CUPS

PREP TIME: 5 minutes

TOTAL COOK TIME:
40 minutes

APPROX. PRESSURE BUILD:
23 to 28 minutes

PRESSURE COOK: 0 minutes

PRESSURE RELEASE:
8 minutes

About 8 cups mixed
vegetable scraps

10 cups water

Don't throw those veggie scraps away! Did you know that you can save all your vegetable peels and trimmings to use for homemade vegetable broth? I save all these scraps (carrot and onion peels, parsley stems, celery leaves—you name it!) in a gallon-size plastic bag in my freezer. When it's about two-thirds full, I dump it into my pressure cooker with some water and make a batch of broth to use for soups, gravies, and other recipes.

1. Dump the vegetable scraps into the pressure cooker pot, then cover with the water, making sure the water does not exceed your pot's maximum fill line (if it does, you need to reduce the recipe quantity based on your pot's capacity).

2. Close and lock the pressure cooker lid, make sure the pressure/steam-release switch is set to sealing, and set the cooking time to 0 minutes at high/normal pressure (if using an electric pressure cooker; for stovetop pressure cookers, heat over a burner on high heat, then immediately remove the pot from the heat once the pot has reached pressure). It will take 23 to 28 minutes for the pot to come to pressure before the cooking time begins.

3. Allow the pressure to release from the pot naturally for 5 minutes before releasing the remaining pressure using the manufacturer's quick-release method (which will take an additional 3 to 4 minutes).

4. Set a colander over a large bowl and pour in the contents of the pot. Discard the solids.

5. Allow the broth to cool for about 20 minutes, then transfer to the fridge to cool completely. Portion into glass jars or plastic freezer bags to refrigerate or freeze.

PER SERVING (1 CUP): Calories: 20; Total Fat: 0g; Saturated Fat: 0g; Cholesterol: 0mg; Sodium: 42mg; Carbohydrates: 2g; Fiber: 0g; Protein: 2g

COOKING TIP

Don't leave your broth in the pot to natural release for too long, or it can become overdone and end up with a burnt flavor. Make sure to release the pressure when it's time and remove the broth from the hot pot.

Chicken Broth

DAIRY-FREE • GLUTEN-FREE • NUT-FREE • MAKES ABOUT 10 CUPS

PREP TIME: 5 minutes

TOTAL COOK TIME: 1 hour 35 minutes

APPROX. PRESSURE BUILD: 25 minutes

PRESSURE COOK: 40 minutes

PRESSURE RELEASE: 30 minutes

2½ pounds bone-in, skin-on chicken parts

1 onion, peeled and quartered

1 celery stalk, cut into 2-inch pieces

1 carrot, peeled and cut into 2-inch pieces

½ teaspoon whole black peppercorns

1 bay leaf

10 cups water

Compared with preparing it the traditional way in a stockpot on the stove, chicken broth made in the pressure cooker takes about half the time and requires much less maintenance. I love having homemade chicken broth in my freezer to use as needed—it makes recipes taste so much better than using canned broth.

1. Put the chicken, onion, celery, carrots, peppercorns, and bay leaf in the pressure cooker pot, then cover with the water, making sure the water does not exceed your pot's maximum fill line (if it does, you need to reduce the recipe quantity based on your pot's capacity).

2. Close and lock the pressure cooker lid, make sure the pressure/steam-release switch is set to sealing, and set the cooking time to 40 minutes at high/normal pressure (if using an electric pressure cooker; for stovetop pressure cookers, heat over a burner on high heat, set a timer for 40 minutes after the pot has reached pressure, then reduce the heat to low). It will take about 25 minutes for the pot to come to pressure before the cooking time begins.

3. Allow the pressure to release from the pot naturally, which will take about 30 minutes. When the pressure has released from the pot, tap or lightly shake the pot before removing the lid to pop any trapped steam bubbles that may be below the food's surface (chicken broth can create a layer of fat on top that may trap steam).
4. Set a colander over a large bowl and pour in the contents of the pot. Discard the solids.
5. Allow the broth to cool for about 30 minutes, then skim and discard the layer of fat on the surface. Transfer to the refrigerator to cool completely. Portion into glass jars or plastic freezer bags to refrigerate or freeze.

PER SERVING (1 CUP): Calories: 35; Total Fat: 1g; Saturated Fat: 0g; Cholesterol: 9mg; Sodium: 54mg; Carbohydrates: 1g; Fiber: 0g; Protein: 5g

LEFTOVER TIP

I freeze my homemade broth in portions to use as needed. I fill quart-size freezer bags with 1- and 2-cup portions of broth, then lay them flat to freeze, as this saves space. I also freeze several ¼-cup portions in silicone muffin pans, then pop them out and store them in gallon-size freezer bags to defrost small amounts as needed.

Country Sausage Gravy

30 MINUTES • NUT-FREE • SERVES 6

PREP TIME: 5 minutes

TOTAL COOK TIME:
30 minutes

APPROX. PRESSURE BUILD:
5 to 6 minutes

PRESSURE COOK: 3 minutes

PRESSURE RELEASE:
10 minutes

1 pound pork
breakfast sausage

¼ cup chicken broth,
store-bought or homemade
(page 170)

½ cup all-purpose flour

3 cups milk

1 teaspoon salt

½ teaspoon freshly ground
black pepper

¼ teaspoon garlic powder

¼ teaspoon onion powder

⅛ teaspoon dried sage

There is nothing like a creamy, white sausage gravy. We love to make this to serve with biscuits for breakfast, but it is also a yummy topping for chicken-fried steak and mashed potatoes.

1. Select the sauté function on the pressure cooker (if using an electric pressure cooker; for stovetop pressure cookers, heat over a burner on medium-high heat). Add the sausage to the pot and sauté for 5 minutes, stirring until evenly browned and crumbled. Press cancel or turn off the burner.

2. Pour the chicken broth into the pot and scrape the bottom of the pot with a wooden spoon to loosen any browned bits.

3. Close and lock the pressure cooker lid, make sure the pressure/steam-release switch is set to sealing, and set the cooking time to 3 minutes at high/normal pressure (if using an electric pressure cooker; for stovetop pressure cookers, heat over a burner on high heat, set a timer for 3 minutes after the pot has reached pressure, then reduce the heat to low). It will take 5 to 6 minutes for the pot to come to pressure before the cooking time begins.

4. After the pressure cooking time ends, electric pressure cookers will automatically turn off their heat (stovetop pressure cookers must be removed from the heat). Allow the pressure to release from the pot naturally for 10 minutes before releasing the remaining pressure using the manufacturer's quick-release method.

5. Open the lid, select the sauté function on the pot again, and stir the flour into the sausage mixture. Stir in the milk, salt, pepper, garlic powder, onion powder, and sage.

6. Simmer, stirring, until the sauce thickens, about 5 minutes, then press cancel or turn off the burner.

PER SERVING: Calories: 288; Total Fat: 19g; Saturated Fat: 7g; Cholesterol: 61mg; Sodium: 743mg; Carbohydrates: 15g; Fiber: 0g; Protein: 17g

Meaty Spaghetti Sauce

DAIRY-FREE • GLUTEN-FREE • NUT-FREE • SERVES 6 TO 8

PREP TIME: 10 minutes

TOTAL COOK TIME:
45 minutes

APPROX. PRESSURE BUILD:
8 minutes

PRESSURE COOK: 15 minutes

PRESSURE RELEASE:
10 minutes

1 pound ground beef

1 medium onion, chopped

4 garlic cloves,
finely chopped

¼ cup dry red wine

10 to 12 tomatoes, chopped

¼ cup tomato paste

1 teaspoon dried basil

1 teaspoon salt

½ teaspoon dried oregano

¼ teaspoon freshly ground
black pepper

This homemade pasta sauce it great to make as a big batch and store in the fridge for quick meals as needed. Our kids love it with any type of pasta that we have on hand, and it makes things easier on busy nights. Serve some garlic bread and a salad on the side and you have a complete meal that pleases everyone.

1. Select the sauté function on the pressure cooker (if using an electric pressure cooker; for stovetop pressure cookers, heat over a burner on medium-high heat). Sauté the ground beef and onion in the pot for 5 minutes. Add the garlic and sauté for 2 more minutes.

2. Pour the red wine into the pot and scrape the bottom of the pot with a wooden spoon to loosen any browned bits. Simmer for another 2 minutes, then press cancel or turn off the burner.

3. Add the tomatoes, tomato paste, basil, salt, oregano, and pepper to the pot and stir well.

4. Close and lock the pressure cooker lid, make sure the pressure/steam-release switch is set to sealing, and set the cooking time to 15 minutes at high/normal pressure (if using an electric pressure cooker; for stovetop pressure cookers, heat over a burner on high heat, set a timer for 15 minutes after the pot has reached pressure, then reduce the heat to low). It will take about 8 minutes for the pot to come to pressure before the cooking time begins.

5. After the pressure cooking time ends, electric pressure cookers will automatically turn off their heat (stovetop pressure cookers must be removed from the heat). Allow the pressure to release from the pot naturally for 10 minutes before releasing the remaining pressure using the manufacturer's quick-release method.

6. Open the pot and stir the sauce.

PER SERVING: Calories: 179; Total Fat: 6g; Saturated Fat: 2g; Cholesterol: 47mg; Sodium: 469mg; Carbohydrates: 14g; Fiber: 4g; Protein: 18g

Chipotle Barbecue Sauce

DAIRY-FREE • GLUTEN-FREE • NUT-FREE • VEGAN • MAKES ABOUT 5 CUPS

PREP TIME: 5 minutes

TOTAL COOK TIME: 1 hour

APPROX. PRESSURE BUILD:
12 minutes

PRESSURE COOK: 12 minutes

PRESSURE RELEASE:
30 minutes

½ **medium onion,
coarsely chopped**

**4 canned chipotle chiles in
adobo sauce**

**3 garlic cloves,
coarsely chopped**

4 cups tomato sauce

½ **cup molasses**

½ **cup apple cider vinegar**

**3 teaspoons
ground mustard**

1 teaspoon salt

½ **teaspoon freshly ground
black pepper**

¼ **teaspoon garlic powder**

¼ **teaspoon onion powder**

*Smoky, spicy chipotle is my favorite barbecue
sauce flavor. I enjoy this barbecue sauce on grilled
sausages, smoked brisket, or smoked beef ribs with
potato salad and baked beans on the side. It's also
delicious on grilled chicken and smoked turkey.*

1. Purée the onion, chipotle chiles, and garlic cloves in
   a food processor or blender. Transfer to the pressure
   cooker pot.
2. Add the tomato sauce, molasses, and apple cider vinegar to the pot and mix well.
3. Stir in the ground mustard, salt, pepper, garlic powder,
   and onion powder.
4. Close and lock the pressure cooker lid, make sure the
   pressure/steam-release switch is set to sealing, and set
   the cooking time to 12 minutes at high/normal pressure (if using an electric pressure cooker; for stovetop
   pressure cookers, heat over a burner on high heat, set
   a timer for 12 minutes after the pot has reached pressure, then reduce the heat to low). It will take about
   12 minutes for the pot to come to pressure before the
   cooking time begins.
5. After the pressure cooking time ends, electric pressure
   cookers will automatically turn off their heat (stovetop
   pressure cookers must be removed from the heat). Allow
   the pressure to release from the pot naturally, which will
   take about 30 minutes.
6. Open the lid and allow the sauce to cool before storing
   in glass jars in the refrigerator.

PER SERVING (¼ CUP): Calories: 51; Total Fat: 0g; Saturated Fat:
0g; Cholesterol: 0mg; Sodium: 176mg; Carbohydrates: 11g; Fiber: 1g;
Protein: 1g

Fresh Berry Compote

30 MINUTES · DAIRY-FREE · GLUTEN-FREE · NUT-FREE · VEGAN
MAKES ABOUT 2 CUPS

PREP TIME: 5 minutes

TOTAL COOK TIME:
30 minutes

APPROX. PRESSURE BUILD:
6 minutes

PRESSURE COOK: 1 minute

PRESSURE RELEASE:
10 minutes

1 pound fresh blueberries,
raspberries, blackberries,
and/or sliced strawberries

¼ cup sugar

1 teaspoon grated
lemon zest

2 tablespoons fresh
lemon juice

INGREDIENT TIP

For a flavor variation, use
orange zest and juice instead
of lemon.

If you're unfamiliar with the term, a compote is simply a sauce of fruit stewed in syrup. It can be served on desserts (like the New York–Style Cheesecake on page 188), with oatmeal (like the 5-Ingredient Cinnamon and Brown Sugar Oatmeal on page 28), mixed into yogurt, on pancakes, and more. This recipe is completely customizable based on the different berries you choose.

1. Put the berries in the pressure cooker pot and sprinkle the sugar evenly over them. Let sit for 10 minutes.
2. Stir in the lemon zest and juice.
3. Close and lock the pressure cooker lid, make sure the pressure/steam-release switch is set to sealing, and set the cooking time to 1 minute at high/normal pressure (if using an electric pressure cooker; for stovetop pressure cookers, heat over a burner on high heat, set a timer for 1 minute after the pot has reached pressure, then reduce the heat to low). It will take about 6 minutes for the pot to come to pressure before the cooking time begins.
4. After the pressure cooking time ends, electric pressure cookers will automatically turn off their heat (stovetop pressure cookers must be removed from the heat). Allow the pressure to release from the pot naturally for 10 minutes before releasing the remaining pressure using the manufacturer's quick-release method.
5. Remove the lid and stir the compote. Cool and serve immediately as a topping for breakfasts or desserts, or store in jars in the refrigerator if you plan to serve it later.

PER SERVING (¼ CUP): Calories: 57; Total Fat: 0g; Saturated Fat: 0g; Cholesterol: 0mg; Sodium: 1mg; Carbohydrates: 15g; Fiber: 1g; Protein: 1g

12

DESSERT

Peanut Butter Pudding

30 MINUTES • GLUTEN-FREE • VEGETARIAN • SERVES 4

PREP TIME: 5 minutes
TOTAL COOK TIME: 20 minutes
APPROX. PRESSURE BUILD: 5 minutes
PRESSURE COOK: 8 minutes
PRESSURE RELEASE: 1 minute

1 cup milk

1 cup half-and-half

⅓ cup sugar

2 tablespoons cornstarch

¼ teaspoon salt

½ cup creamy peanut butter

1 teaspoon vanilla extract

1 cup water

We are big peanut butter fans in our family, so homemade peanut butter pudding is a treat we make whenever we are feeling the craving. It is easier than you might think to make homemade pudding, and it's made with ingredients you probably already have in your pantry.

1. Select the sauté function on the pressure cooker (if using an electric pressure cooker; for stovetop pressure cookers, heat over a burner on medium-high heat). Whisk the milk, half-and-half, sugar, cornstarch, and salt together in the pressure cooker pot. Simmer, whisking frequently until it starts to bubble, about 7 minutes.

2. Whisk in the peanut butter and vanilla until the peanut butter is melted and mixed in completely. Press cancel or turn off the burner. Transfer the pudding to a heat-safe bowl (I use a 7-cup glass bowl) and cover with aluminum foil.

3. When the pot is cool enough to handle, wash and dry it. Pour the water into the pressure cooker pot and place a steamer rack trivet in the bottom. Place the bowl of pudding on the trivet.

4. Close and lock the pressure cooker lid, make sure the pressure/steam-release switch is set to sealing, and set the cooking time to 8 minutes at high/normal pressure (if using an electric pressure cooker; for stovetop pressure cookers, heat over a burner on high heat, set a timer for 8 minutes after the pot has reached pressure, then reduce the heat to low). It will take about 5 minutes for the pot to come to pressure before the cooking time begins.

5. After the pressure cooking time ends, electric pressure cookers will automatically turn off their heat (stovetop pressure cookers must be removed from the heat). Release the pressure using the manufacturer's quick-release method.

6. Carefully remove the bowl from the pressure cooker and stir the pudding. Let it cool on the counter, then serve.

PER SERVING: Calories: 379; Total Fat: 24g; Saturated Fat: 9g; Cholesterol: 27mg; Sodium: 349mg; Carbohydrates: 32g; Fiber: 2g; Protein: 12g

COOKING TIP

See the Cooking Tip on page 29 for how to use a bakeware sling.

Walnut Brownies

VEGETARIAN • SERVES 6

PREP TIME: 10 minutes
TOTAL COOK TIME: 1 hour 10 minutes
APPROX. PRESSURE BUILD: 8 minutes
PRESSURE COOK: 50 minutes
PRESSURE RELEASE: 10 minutes

Nonstick cooking spray

1½ cups water

1 cup sugar

½ cup all-purpose flour

⅓ cup unsweetened cocoa powder

¼ teaspoon baking powder

8 tablespoons (1 stick) unsalted butter, melted

2 large eggs

½ teaspoon vanilla extract

½ cup chopped walnuts

I've adapted the popular classic brownies recipe from my blog for the pressure cooker. This pot-in-pot brownie recipe is foolproof and can be customized with different nuts and chocolate or other flavored candy chips. No matter which variation, you'll get that perfect dense-but-moist-in-the-center brownie every time.

1. Spray a heat-safe bowl (I use a 7-cup glass bowl) with nonstick cooking spray.
2. Pour the water into the pressure cooker pot and place a steamer rack trivet in the bottom.
3. In a medium bowl, whisk together the sugar, flour, cocoa powder, and baking powder.
4. In a large bowl, whisk together the melted butter, eggs, and vanilla.
5. Add the dry ingredients to the wet ingredients and mix until well combined. Fold in the chopped walnuts.
6. Pour the batter into the prepared heat-safe bowl and smooth the top with a spatula. Lay a paper towel over the top of the bowl (this will help catch excess moisture from the steam inside the pot), then cover the paper towel and bowl loosely with aluminum foil. Place the bowl on the trivet inside the pot.

INGREDIENT TIPS

＊ It is important to use real, unsalted butter for this recipe and not margarine, otherwise the consistency will not be the same.

＊ You can substitute chopped pecans for the walnuts if you prefer, or skip the nuts altogether.

7. Close and lock the pressure cooker lid, make sure the pressure/steam-release switch is set to sealing, and set the cooking time to 50 minutes at high/normal pressure (if using an electric pressure cooker; for stovetop pressure cookers, heat over a burner on high heat, set a timer for 50 minutes after the pot has reached pressure, then reduce the heat to low). It will take about 8 minutes for the pot to come to pressure before cooking time begins.

8. After the pressure cooking time ends, electric pressure cookers will automatically turn off their heat (stovetop pressure cookers must be removed from the heat). Allow the pressure to release from the pot naturally for 10 minutes before releasing the remaining pressure using the manufacturer's quick-release method.

9. Carefully remove the bowl from the pot and cool on a wire rack before slicing.

PER SERVING: Calories: 407; Total Fat: 25g; Saturated Fat: 12g; Cholesterol: 103mg; Sodium: 134mg; Carbohydrates: 45g; Fiber: 3g; Protein: 6g

COOKING TIP

See the Cooking Tip on page 29 for how to use a bakeware sling.

Red Velvet Cake Bites

NUT-FREE • VEGETARIAN • MAKES 14 CAKE BITES

PREP TIME: 10 minutes

TOTAL COOK TIME: 1 hour

APPROX. PRESSURE BUILD:
7 minutes

PRESSURE COOK: 12 minutes

PRESSURE RELEASE:
30 minutes

Nonstick cooking spray

1 cup water

1½ cups all-purpose flour

⅓ cup unsweetened
cocoa powder

1 teaspoon baking powder

1 teaspoon baking soda

¼ teaspoon salt

¾ cup granulated sugar

½ cup buttermilk

4 tablespoons (½ stick)
plus 2 tablespoons unsalted
butter, at room
temperature, divided

1 large egg

2 tablespoons plain
unsweetened Greek yogurt

1 teaspoon red food
coloring

1 cup confectioners' sugar

4 ounces cream cheese, at
room temperature

1 tablespoon heavy cream

¼ teaspoon vanilla extract

Yes, you can make moist and delicious red velvet cake in a pressure cooker! Silicone egg-bite molds are great for mini cupcakes and cake bites like this recipe. You can serve these at a party as mini cake bites or on sticks as cake pops, as they are the perfect size for party snacking.

1. Spray the cups of two silicone egg molds with nonstick cooking spray.
2. Pour the water into the pressure cooker pot and place a steamer rack trivet in the bottom.
3. In a medium bowl, whisk together the flour, cocoa powder, baking powder, baking soda, and salt.
4. In a large bowl, beat together the granulated sugar, buttermilk, 4 tablespoons of butter, egg, and yogurt with a hand mixer until smooth.
5. Add the dry ingredients to the wet ingredients and mix with the hand mixer until well combined. Add the red food coloring and beat until the color is fully incorporated into the batter
6. Fill the cups of the egg molds halfway with batter. Lay a paper towel over the top of each mold (this will help catch excess moisture from the steam inside the pot), then cover the paper towel and egg bite molds loosely with aluminum foil.
7. Stack the two molds on top of each other and place on the trivet inside the pot.

8. Close and lock the pressure cooker lid, make sure the pressure/steam-release switch is set to sealing, and set the cooking time to 12 minutes at high/normal pressure (if using an electric pressure cooker; for stovetop pressure cookers, heat over a burner on high heat, set a timer for 12 minutes after the pot has reached pressure, then reduce the heat to low). It will take about 7 minutes for the pot to come to pressure before cooking time begins.

9. After the pressure cooking time ends, electric pressure cookers will automatically turn off their heat (stovetop pressure cookers must be removed from the heat). Allow the pressure to release from the pot naturally, which will take about 30 minutes.

10. Remove the molds from the pressure cooker and cool on a wire rack before using a spoon or butter knife to remove the cake bites from the molds.

11. While the cake bites are cooling, in a small bowl, whip the confectioners' sugar, cream cheese, remaining 2 tablespoons of butter, heavy cream, and vanilla together with the hand mixer until fluffy, about 1 minute.

12. Dip each cake bite halfway into the cream cheese frosting.

PER SERVING (1 CAKE BITE): Calories: 214; Total Fat: 9g; Saturated Fat: 6g; Cholesterol: 37mg; Sodium: 209mg; Carbohydrates: 32g; Fiber: 1g; Protein: 3g

Lemon Bundt Cake

NUT-FREE • VEGETARIAN • SERVES 8

PREP TIME: 10 minutes

TOTAL COOK TIME: 1 hour 10 minutes

APPROX. PRESSURE BUILD: 6 to 7 minutes

PRESSURE COOK: 35 minutes

PRESSURE RELEASE: 30 minutes

Nonstick cooking spray

2 cups all-purpose flour

1 teaspoon baking powder

1 teaspoon baking soda

¼ teaspoon salt

1 cup granulated sugar

1 cup plain unsweetened Greek yogurt

8 tablespoons (1 stick) unsalted butter, at room temperature

1 large egg

3 tablespoons fresh lemon juice, divided

1 tablespoon grated lemon zest

1 cup water

1 cup confectioners' sugar

1 tablespoon half-and-half

This Bundt cake serves eight, but lemon lovers will try to sneak extra servings of this light and moist cake. It is topped with a creamy lemon glaze but isn't overly sweet. This cake keeps well, and the leftovers are great with coffee for breakfast.

1. Spray a 6-cup Bundt pan with nonstick cooking spray.
2. In a medium bowl, whisk together the flour, baking powder, baking soda, and salt.
3. In a large bowl, beat together the granulated sugar, yogurt, butter, egg, 2 tablespoons of lemon juice, and lemon zest with a hand mixer until smooth.
4. Add the dry ingredients to the wet ingredients and mix with the hand mixer until well combined.
5. Pour the batter into the prepared Bundt pan. Lay a paper towel over the top of the pan (this will help catch excess moisture from the steam inside the pot), then cover the paper towel and pan loosely with aluminum foil.
6. Pour the water into the pressure cooker pot and place a steamer rack trivet in the bottom. Place the foil-covered Bundt pan on the trivet.
7. Close and lock the pressure cooker lid, make sure the pressure/steam-release switch is set to sealing, and set the cooking time to 35 minutes at high/normal pressure (if using an electric pressure cooker; for stovetop pressure cookers, heat over a burner on high heat, set a timer for 35 minutes after the pot has reached pressure, then reduce the heat to low). It will take 6 to 7 minutes for the pot to come to pressure before the cooking time begins.

8. After the pressure cooking time ends, electric pressure cookers will automatically turn off their heat (stovetop pressure cookers must be removed from the heat). Allow the pressure to release from the pot naturally, about 30 minutes.

9. Carefully remove the Bundt pan from the pot and cool on a wire rack.

10. While the cake is cooling, in a small bowl, whisk together the confectioners' sugar, half-and-half, and remaining 1 tablespoon of lemon juice to make the lemon glaze.

11. When cool enough to handle, invert the pan over a serving plate and remove the cake. Drizzle with the lemon glaze.

PER SERVING: Calories: 414; Total Fat: 14g; Saturated Fat: 9g; Cholesterol: 56mg; Sodium: 342mg; Carbohydrates: 66g; Fiber: 1g; Protein: 7g

INGREDIENT TIPS

* "Baked" goods prepared in the pressure cooker are technically cooked with hot steam instead of hot air as in an oven. As a result, cakes and breads will end up very moist, but with a denser texture. For fluffier "baked" goods in the pressure cooker, and to prevent them from being too dense, be sure to properly measure your flour. Instead of scooping flour out of its container with a measuring cup, spoon the flour into your measuring cup, then gently level it with the back of a knife (as opposed to packing it down).

* See the Cooking Tip on page 29 for how to use a bakeware sling.

New York–Style Cheesecake

NUT-FREE • VEGETARIAN • **SERVES 8**

PREP TIME: 20 minutes

TOTAL COOK TIME: 1 hour

APPROX. PRESSURE BUILD:
7 to 8 minutes

PRESSURE COOK:
35 minutes

PRESSURE RELEASE:
10 minutes

Nonstick cooking spray

1 cup graham
cracker crumbs

4 tablespoons (½ stick)
unsalted butter, melted

1 tablespoon brown sugar

Pinch salt

2 (8-ounce) packages
cream cheese, at room
temperature

½ cup heavy cream

½ cup granulated sugar

3 large eggs

1½ teaspoons cornstarch

1 teaspoon vanilla extract

½ teaspoon almond extract

1½ cups water

Cheesecake is unbelievably easy to make in the pressure cooker. Not only does it cook quickly, but it cooks perfectly in the moist, high-pressure environment without the frequent monitoring required for oven-baked cheesecake. The 7-inch springform pan that fits into 6- and 8-quart pressure cookers makes a slightly smaller cake, which makes it more convenient for everyday desserts and not just for a big party—in case you needed an excuse to make a cheesecake! Serve the cheesecake by itself or topped with Fresh Berry Compote (page 177).

1. Spray a 7-inch springform pan with nonstick spray.
2. In a small bowl, mix the graham cracker crumbs, butter, brown sugar, and salt until all the crumbs are moistened. Press the graham cracker mixture into the bottom and partway up the sides of the prepared springform pan. Place the pan in the freezer for 15 minutes to set.
3. Meanwhile, in a medium bowl, beat together the cream cheese, heavy cream, granulated sugar, eggs, cornstarch, vanilla extract, and almond extract with a hand mixer until well mixed. Pour the cream cheese mixture into the crust in the springform pan.
4. Pour the water into the pressure cooker pot and place a steamer rack trivet in the bottom. Place the uncovered springform pan on the trivet.

5. Close and lock the pressure cooker lid, make sure the pressure/steam-release switch is set to sealing, and set the cooking time to 35 minutes at high/normal pressure (if using an electric pressure cooker; for stovetop pressure cookers, heat over a burner on high heat, set a timer for 35 minutes after the pot has reached pressure, then reduce the heat to low). It will take 7 to 8 minutes for the pot to come to pressure before the cooking time begins.

6. After the pressure cooking time ends, electric pressure cookers will automatically turn off their heat (stovetop pressure cookers must be removed from the heat). Allow the pressure to release from the pot naturally for 10 minutes before releasing the remaining pressure using the manufacturer's quick-release method.

7. Open the lid and use a paper towel to absorb any water that may have accumulated on the top of the cheesecake from the steam.

8. Carefully remove the pan from the pot and cool on a wire rack on the counter for 30 minutes before transferring to the fridge to chill for 8 hours (or overnight).

9. To serve, remove the outer ring of the springform pan and slice.

PER SERVING: Calories: 428; Total Fat: 34g; Saturated Fat: 20g; Cholesterol: 168mg; Sodium: 354mg; Carbohydrates: 25g; Fiber: 1g; Protein: 8g

Apple Crisp

30 MINUTES • NUT-FREE • VEGETARIAN • SERVES 6

PREP TIME: 10 minutes
TOTAL COOK TIME: 10 minutes
APPROX. PRESSURE BUILD: 8 minutes
PRESSURE COOK: 1 minute
PRESSURE RELEASE: 1 minute

8 small apples, cored and sliced

1 cup water

½ tablespoon fresh lemon juice

½ cup plus 2 tablespoons brown sugar, divided

¾ teaspoon ground cinnamon, divided

1 cup quick oats

¼ cup all-purpose flour

8 tablespoons (1 stick) unsalted butter, melted

Pinch salt

If you have an excess of apples, this dessert can be whipped up quickly in your pressure cooker along with some basic pantry ingredients. It's sweet and satisfying, like apple pie in a bowl. Serve warm on its own or topped with a scoop of vanilla ice cream.

1. Put the apple slices in the pressure cooker pot. Add the water, lemon juice, 2 tablespoons of brown sugar, and ¼ teaspoon of cinnamon and stir well.

2. Close and lock the pressure cooker lid, make sure the pressure/steam-release switch is set to sealing, and set the cooking time to 1 minute at high/normal pressure (if using an electric pressure cooker; for stovetop pressure cookers, heat over a burner on high heat, set a timer for 1 minute after the pot has reached pressure, then reduce the heat to low). It will take about 8 minutes for the pot to come to pressure before the cooking time begins.

3. Meanwhile, in a medium bowl, combine the oats, flour, butter, remaining ½ cup of brown sugar, remaining ½ teaspoon of cinnamon, and salt, stirring until well blended and crumbly.

4. After the pressure cooking time ends, electric pressure cookers will automatically turn off their heat (stovetop pressure cookers must be removed from the heat). Release the pressure using the manufacturer's quick-release method.

5. Open the lid and stir the apples gently. Pour the oatmeal crumble evenly on top of the apples and let it sit for 1 minute to warm the crumble topping.

PER SERVING: Calories: 371; Total Fat: 16g; Saturated Fat: 10g; Cholesterol: 41mg; Sodium: 142mg; Carbohydrates: 58g; Fiber: 8g; Protein: 3g

Measurement Conversions

VOLUME EQUIVALENTS (LIQUID)

US STANDARD	US STANDARD (OUNCES)	METRIC (APPROXIMATE)
2 tablespoons	1 fl. oz.	30 mL
¼ cup	2 fl. oz.	60 mL
½ cup	4 fl. oz.	120 mL
1 cup	8 fl. oz.	240 mL
1½ cups	12 fl. oz.	355 mL
2 cups or 1 pint	16 fl. oz.	475 mL
4 cups or 1 quart	32 fl. oz.	1 L
1 gallon	128 fl. oz.	4 L

OVEN TEMPERATURES

FAHRENHEIT (F)	CELSIUS (C) (APPROXIMATE)
250°	120°
300°	150°
325°	165°
350°	180°
375°	190°
400°	200°
425°	220°
450°	230°

VOLUME EQUIVALENTS (DRY)

US STANDARD	METRIC (APPROXIMATE)
⅛ teaspoon	0.5 mL
¼ teaspoon	1 mL
½ teaspoon	2 mL
¾ teaspoon	4 mL
1 teaspoon	5 mL
1 tablespoon	15 mL
¼ cup	59 mL
⅓ cup	79 mL
½ cup	118 mL
⅔ cup	156 mL
¾ cup	177 mL
1 cup	235 mL
2 cups or 1 pint	475 mL
3 cups	700 mL
4 cups or 1 quart	1 L

WEIGHT EQUIVALENTS

US STANDARD	METRIC (APPROXIMATE)
½ ounce	15 g
1 ounce	30 g
2 ounces	60 g
4 ounces	115 g
8 ounces	225 g
12 ounces	340 g
16 ounces or 1 pound	455 g

Index

Acknowledgments

I WOULD LIKE TO THANK the following people:

My mother and father, for teaching me how to cook, being my biggest fans, and always supporting my dreams. I wish there was a way I could repay you for all you've done and all you continue to do for me.

My husband, Nik, for being my partner in life. I love you more than I have room to express, but I hope you know that this book would not be possible without your support and partnership.

My sons, Grayson and Sawyer, for encouraging me to shoot for the stars, and for putting up with breakfast foods and appetizers for every meal of the day for the weeks I was working on those chapters.

My siblings, granddaddy, nieces and nephews, aunts and uncles, and cousins, for their support, honesty, advice, and love. I can always count on you and appreciate that more than you know.

My neighbors, especially the Henderson and Meyer families, for being my taste testers and taking so much food off my hands during the development of the recipes in this book. My fridge (and waistline) wouldn't have been able to handle it without you!

My friend, Melissa, for her friendship and support, and her time and effort beta testing some of these recipes.

The Allrecipes Allstars program and community of home cooks, for their friendship, and for always challenging me to expand my abilities as a cook and recipe developer.

My dear friends, Jen, Arnali, Matt, and the TKN girls for their love, friendship, and support. I'm grateful to have you in my life.

The blogging community, for consistently inspiring me to create and to build a living out of what I love to do.

The team at Callisto Media, for giving me the chance to write my first book and coaching this newbie author every step of the way. I am thrilled that we get to bring these recipes to the world together.

About the Author

RAMONA CRUZ-PETERS is the founder and writer of *Fab Everyday*, a lifestyle website and social media presence that reaches more than 2 million people per month. Written from her point of view as a working mom who can appreciate both the simple and fabulous things in life, Fab Everyday operates on the belief that life can be lived fabulously (even with a busy schedule, two messy boys, and operating on a budget). After graduating from UCLA with a degree in sociology, Ramona began her communications career in information technology and social media at Myspace, where she spent five years. Following that, she worked in marketing and communications for both private and nonprofit organizations (one of which she led to a social media award for the *Austin-American Statesman*), until leaving the corporate world to manage Fab Everyday full-time in 2018. Ramona's recipes and projects have been featured in *Allrecipes Magazine*, *Good Housekeeping*, *BuzzFeed*, *POPSUGAR*, *Atlanta Parent*, *Apartment Therapy*, and more. Born in England and raised in Southern California, Ramona is a (very) busy thirtysomething mom of two sons (10-year-old Grayson and 7-year-old Sawyer) living with her husband, children, and two pug dogs near Austin, Texas. Keep up with Ramona and all her recipes and lifestyle tips at FabEveryday.com and @FabEverydayblog on Facebook, Instagram, Pinterest, and Twitter.

CPSIA information can be obtained
at www.ICGtesting.com
Printed in the USA
LVHW071352090220
646022LV00003B/1